Commercial Real Estate Power Brokers

Commercial Real Estate
Power Brokers

INTERVIEWS WITH THE BEST IN THE BUSINESS

Jim Gillespie

First published by Advanced Commercial Real Estate Coaching in 2018
Copyright © Jim Gillespie, 2018
First Edition
ISBN-13: 9781984194855
ISBN-10: 1984194852
Library of Congress Control Number: 2017918728
CreateSpace Independent Publishing Platform
North Charleston, South Carolina

Dedication

To my parents, Jim and Veronica Gillespie:
Thank you for all the never-ending love you constantly gave to me.
I am honored to have been your son.

Table of Contents

Foreword ·ix

Introduction· ·xi

Interview 1: How to Prospect Powerfully in Commercial
Real Estate Brokerage · 1

Interview 2: Building Solid Relationships With Your
Commercial Real Estate Clients· · · · · · · · · · · · · · · · · 44

Interview 3: Making Powerful Presentations That Will Get
You More Listings · 89

Interview 4: Designing Your Brokerage Business to
Maximize Success · 139

Interview 5: Beating Your Commercial Real Estate
Competitors for the Business · · · · · · · · · · · · · · · · · · · 191

Epilogue· 241

About the Author· 245

Foreword

When I first learned that Jim Gillespie was going to begin interviewing top commercial real estate brokers years ago, I thought that this was a great idea. How many of us in commercial real estate have wished, over the years, that we could hear top brokers telling us their innermost strategies for commercial real estate brokerage success? For the most part, within our industry, it's rare to even have a top broker within our own office be willing to tell us what they know, and now Jim has completed more than 140 interviews with these top brokers, and five of his all-time best interviews are now contained within this book.

I was actually the first broker that Jim interviewed during one of his teleconferences back when he first began doing this. But since then, Jim has now covered many different subjects during his interviews, and he's chosen his brokers for these interviews according to their own level of expertise on the specific subject. You'll be hearing from some of the best brokers in the business in this book, including hearing from top members of both SIOR and CCIM, and these are all individuals who have become truly exceptional brokers within our industry.

I've subscribed to Jim's free E-newsletter for many years now, and have read many of his more than 400 commercial real estate training articles, and have watched his commercial real estate training videos as well. When doing this, and even during the times that Jim has interviewed me during his teleconferences, it's been clear to me that Jim has a solid understanding of what we as commercial real estate brokers need to know, in order to achieve what we truly want in our brokerage businesses.

During these interviews contained in this book, Jim not only does a good job of bringing out the information that you'll want to learn about, he does a good job, as well, of sharing his own wisdom and expertise from his decades of experience as a broker, coach, and trainer in our industry, so that you'll gain the most from each interview.

I'm confident that you'll enjoy reading these interviews, and that you'll gain insight from them that will help you become more productive in your brokerage business.

Stan Mullin, SIOR, CCIM
Past President, Society of Industrial and Office Realtors
Past President, AIR CRE

Introduction

When I created commercial real estate coaching back in the 1990s, I recognized that there was a need that wasn't being fulfilled within our industry. Still, even to this day, brokers constantly tell me that they're lacking good training within their own companies, and that oftentimes their training consists of being given a desk and a phone, and being told to pick up the phone and start calling people.

In addition, I noticed that there was often very little sharing of both information and success strategies going on among brokers within their own offices. Brokers are so busy working on transactions, and they oftentimes don't want to share their success strategies with other brokers, because they're afraid that doing so may cause them to then lose business to these brokers.

So in the early 2000s, I recognized the need for brokers to begin learning from other brokers within our industry, and I began interviewing some of the best brokers in the business...brokers like the ones you'll be hearing from within this book.

But now after having done more than 140 interviews with these top-producing brokers, my clients have continually asked me how I've made this happen. They've asked me questions like, "How do you get these top-producing brokers to bare their souls and tell us everything they're doing all the time? I can't even get the brokers in my own office to tell me anything!"

With this in mind, it hasn't been easy for me to find these brokers, but I've done it. I tell my clients that the brokers I'm looking for are the ones who are producing truly outstanding results, who are engaging, and who won't put an audience to sleep. In addition, I need them to be people who would be willing to openly share everything they're doing to produce such outstanding results within their own brokerage businesses. So in my opinion, this narrows it down to being maybe 2-3% of all of the brokers in our industry who would qualify for me to then interview them.

But whenever I contact a top broker and approach them with the idea of interviewing them, the response that I often get is, "Why in the world would I ever want to do that? Why would I want to teach other brokers what I'm already doing to produce such outstanding results within my own brokerage business?"

So it's been a real journey to find these great brokers who've been willing to share their own expertise with you, and who have been willing to tell you everything they know about what's made them become so outstanding within our industry.

The five brokers who are interviewed within this book represent some of the most outstanding brokers within our industry. In addition, I could call any one of these brokers at anytime and they'd be willing to do another interview with me. So they're outstanding at what they do, and they're both willing and interested in sharing their expertise with other brokers within our industry. In short, they're definitely my kind of brokers!

So when you read my interview with Mike Monteleone, CCIM, the greatest prospector I've ever known, you will see the discipline that he has to never let anything ever get in the way of him getting his prospecting done. In addition, you will read about the specific routine that he goes through every single day to maximize both his productivity, and his prospecting results.

During my interview with William Hugron, SIOR, CCIM, you'll not only learn some solid approaches for building stronger relationships with your clients, you'll read how Willy sometimes even goes the extra mile, and does things like having a chauffeur pick up his client and their spouse in a classic Rolls Royce, taking them out for a lovely night on the town...all paid for by Willy. You can imagine what something like this does towards creating great client loyalty!

With John DeGrinis, SIOR, you'll learn how to become even more effective in your approach to get more listings, and you'll hear about his approach that he refers to as having the pre-meeting...a meeting with the owners ahead of time to bond even deeper with them, which will help you to answer the right questions during your listing presentation, so you'll deliver an even more powerful presentation that will get you the listing.

Then with Scott Lamontagne, he'll tell you how to design your business so that you're maximizing your income, so you begin delegating the activities that are currently sapping your productive time. In addition, Scott will tell you how he and his team have all agreed to pay $1,500.00 fines whenever anyone doesn't get their work done on time, which means that everyone always gets their work done on time.

And finally, you'll hear from Bill Gladstone, SIOR, CCIM, the best marketer I've ever known in commercial real estate brokerage. Bill spends over $100,000.00 a year on marketing, and he has bobblehead dolls made to look like him that he hands out to his clients and prospects as promotional pieces. In addition, Bill will tell you a story about how he sometimes pre-records a video of himself talking, and then during his live listing presentation, he will have a dialogue in front of his owners with the "Bill" that he's pre-recorded in the video, while the video is playing up on the screen in front of everyone in the room. This gets his owners to both smile and laugh during his listing presentation, moving him even closer towards beating all of his competitors to get the listing.

There are many other agents I've interviewed over the years whose interviews I could have easily included within this book, too, but these five interviews I believe do a great job together of covering many areas that are extremely important to commercial real estate brokers.

During these interviews, in addition to discussing the main topic of the interview subject along with the broker, I'll also ask them questions about what they're doing within other areas of their brokerage business, too. When I have direct access to these brokers who are playing the game at this high level, I believe it's important to get all of the great information that I can out of them, because just one thing that they may say on another subject could be something that you may find very important.

So there you have it. What's now left for you to do is to read these interviews, learn from them, and then implement the best of what you've learned into your own brokerage business. With this being said, I wish you all the best of success and enjoyment in reading these interviews, and in taking your commercial real estate brokerage business to the next level!

Jim Gillespie

INTERVIEW 1

How to Prospect Powerfully in Commercial Real Estate Brokerage

Jim: Hi, this is Jim Gillespie, America's Premier Commercial Real Estate Coach℠, located on the web at www.CommercialRealEstateCoach.com. Tonight I'm going to be interviewing our special guest, Mike Monteleone, CCIM, on the subject of prospecting, and then during the middle of our interview I will also then segue into speaking to you directly for about 20 minutes, as there are certain aspects about prospecting that I want to make sure to communicate to you.

So we'll be going for about 90 minutes in total tonight, and with that being said, here's my Introduction for Mike:

Mike Monteleone, CCIM, has closed more than $1.4 billion in real estate transactions during his real estate career. Throughout his career he has sold commercial land, commercial and industrial buildings, apartment buildings, 1031 exchange properties, as well as estate properties.

He's a past recipient of the Small Businessman of the Year award from the City of Los Angeles. He's owned his own real estate brokerage company, and he's trained over 1,000 agents. He's now working for RE/MAX, and he's ranked in the top 1% of all RE/MAX agents in his region, and in the top 2% of all agents selling real estate in North America.

Mike and I have known each other for more than 30 years now, and there is no other broker I've known who is as disciplined and determined to get his prospecting done than Mike.

With that being said, please welcome onto our call tonight, Mike Monteleone.

Mike: Thank you. Gosh, Jim, in listening to that Introduction I find myself asking, "Who is that guy? Is that really me?"

Jim: Yes, it sounds impressive, doesn't it? You've sometimes got to take it all in and acknowledge what you've really accomplished throughout your career.

Mike: No kidding!

Jim: In getting started here, I know how big you are on prospecting and how good you are at getting it done, which is why I wanted to have you specifically on the call here tonight. So let's start off by asking, "How important do you think prospecting is for commercial brokers to develop more business for themselves?"

Mike: It's probably the #1 priority, Jim. I was just thinking about that. As far as where we can generate our real estate business from, really there are just a few ways of doing it. We can either buy it, you can wait for it, or you can go after it. With that in mind, going after the business is not that expensive, compared to buying it. It's something that has been predictable for me, and then I can also track it. The best results I've gotten have been through going after business each and every day by prospecting.

Jim: With that in mind, why do you think it is that so many commercial brokers aren't getting their prospecting done?

Mike: Well, first of all, nobody likes to prospect. I mean I prospect every day and I still don't like prospecting, so that's just the bottom line. We have to get over it. I've done it for so many years and it's automatic after I get rolling on it, but it's intimidating. If you haven't done it before, a lot of people don't know exactly what to say. Maybe they don't have the scripts, or maybe they're not practiced enough.

Rejection is a big one. Some people just need to understand that rejection is not about them, it's about the prospect not being interested in the moment, and yet we could go back to that same prospect three months from now and all of a sudden they have an interest. So you can't let that bother you.

Sometimes agents don't place any value on prospecting. Maybe it's because they've never done it, or they've never really evaluated what the return is on their investment.

Jim: Sure, and actually with you bringing up the subject of rejection and having known you for many years, you mentioned to me years ago how you reframe the rejection with respect to how much money you've just earned from that prospecting call. Talk to us for a minute about that.

Mike: I evaluate every year what every minute of the day is worth in prospecting, Jim. Just to give you an example, last year I was earning about $700.00 an hour for prospecting, from all of the deals I was closing. That averages out to about $73.00 per contact. So when somebody hangs up the phone on me, I really smile and say, "Next!" I'm convinced that the next one will be a "Yes", so I don't worry about it anymore. Because I know if I just do the numbers, there will be the reward at the end.

Jim: I know sometimes you even say to the person, "Thank you, you just made me $73.00!"

Mike: Yes, if I get somebody on the phone, and if they're really angry or whatever, and they shut me down real quick I say, "Thank you. That was $73.00!"

There are times when you just lose it!

Jim: I understand. With all the prospecting you've done for decades now, every now and then you've got to blow off some steam.

Mike: And I don't recommend it. [laughing]

Jim: How much prospecting do you think brokers should be doing in their business every single week?

Mike: In this economy, I have obviously thought maybe three hours a day would be enough, and it's not. I'm upping it another hour. I'd say at least 20 hours a week, and then we'll go from there, Jim. The market and the numbers and everything just aren't the same as it was before, so we have to change. To do this effectively and to make the kind of money that I want to make, it's going to be a minimum of four hours a day.

Jim: For somebody who's been around this business as long as you have saying, "I've got to do 20 hours a week of prospecting," that just says it all right there. I usually tell brokers they ought to be doing at least 10-12 hours a week, but I completely agree with you, Mike. If you're committed to doing 20 hours a week, you're going to produce much better results. But usually I have a tough time even getting brokers to do 10-12 hours a week.

I think sometimes one of the keys can be recognizing how much great activity you have going on. If you don't have the solid amount of activity going on that you really want to be experiencing, then you need to be doing more prospecting.

Mike: Well, you start from an hour a day just to get going on it. It depends on your experience level and what your goals are, and how determined you are. Everybody's different, but you've got to start someplace.

Jim: I agree. I just think it's phenomenal to see that you realize that's what you've got to be doing, because if you're doing it, so many other brokers should really be doing it at that level, too.

In your earlier years in the business, were you always getting your prospecting done, or is this something you've actually gotten better at doing over the years?

Mike: In the early years, I really didn't know what was going to pay me the best for my time. I really didn't do a lot of prospecting until about my third month, when I was then called aside by another broker. When I saw him cranking out deal after deal after deal, he pulled me aside and said, "Mike, would you like to make some big money?", and he taught me how to prospect. After about three months in the business, I really got the message that this was something I needed to do all the time.

Jim: I believe that prospecting is still something that you don't normally want to do, but once you start doing it for 10-15 minutes or so, magically all of a sudden it feels fine, or even like something you're actually enjoying doing, right?

Mike: Exactly. Once you get on a roll, and it's a mindset thing, too. I work on that every day, and I could give you an idea of what I do in the morning just to prepare myself also.

Jim: Please do, because having known you for years, it will be good to hear your preparation routine before doing your prospecting.

Mike: Not everybody's going to follow this routine, but this is what I do that works for me. I'm up at 4:00 a.m., I'm at the gym by 5:30, and at the gym I'm listening to either Napoleon Hill or somebody that is really going to give me some stimulation and motivation. I've also made a recording of my goals, and that's about a 15-minute segment which has everything that I want to accomplish this year in there.

Every day I realize what I'm supposed to be doing, so by the time I get back on the phone, which is at about 7:45 a.m., I then receive a call from my son and we role play for about 30 minutes. We're now role playing scripts and dialogues, and also getting our energy level up and prepared, because I'm usually on the phone by 8:15 a.m. So by 8:15 is when I'm ready to rock and roll!

With my surroundings I make sure I'm prepared, so in the background I usually don't have loud music, but some very fast-paced music in the background so it keeps me stimulated. I built an office, I don't know, Jim, that you've ever seen my office, but it's really all about prospecting. I have mirrors and I make sure I'm always smiling. I stand up and I make sure I don't eat a lot in the morning, just mainly some fruit so I don't get dragged down.

I stand up for usually an hour, and then I take a break, and then I'm back on the phones again. In the background, the music keeps me motivated and I just get into the groove or get into the zone, whatever you want to call it. I don't think about it anymore. The time goes by and I know that I'm doing the right thing, so my mindset is real strong and very positive. Again, I look at $73.00 per contact and then I'm fine.

Jim: I think that is so great that after so many years in the business you're still doing role playing on a regular basis in your preparation. I just realized while you were talking about this that doing that role playing ahead of time probably makes it an easier segue for you to then pick up the phone and make your first real prospecting call, doesn't it?

Mike: Oh absolutely. It's just automatic.

Jim: It's just not that big of a deal when you've been role playing in a safe environment with somebody you know, like your son, and then it's like, "OK, now it's just time to pick up the phone and dial my first prospect for real." It's probably not nearly as big of a deal anymore.

Mike: No, and we throw objections out at each other, too. We make sure that we're able to handle those quickly and then we move on, so it's not that big of a deal.

Jim: How important is it before you pick up the phone and start calling your prospects to actually have their names and their phone numbers right in front of you and ready to go?

Mike: It's critical, because in essence if you're going to be putting in three to four hours a day of prospecting, you certainly want to hit a certain number of people per hour. If you're sitting there trying to figure out who to call, you could waste half an hour to an hour in the process and you're just not going to get the results you're looking for. If you really do plan to get a certain dollar amount out of each hour and every minute, you've got to be prepared.

Jim: Yes, because I know there are many commercial brokers who sit down, they look at the phone, and then they start to try to figure out who they're going to call. Then they'll make the call and immediately afterwards it's like, "OK, who's the next person going to be now?", and then they kind of start going through their database. So there's all this dead time between calls, thinking about who the next call is going to be, which is just not a great place to be. You want to be able to churn the calls out one after another to make the most out of the time you're actually spending doing your prospecting.

Mike: Exactly. I want to just share, and I don't know if I ever mentioned this to you, I hired a gal and I call her a hammer, because basically what she does for me in the time when I'm doing my calls, is she's calling from another phone and she's trying to locate the people that are there. So if she gets somebody that answers, then she faxes or emails over to me while I'm still dialing here, and I have another three or four or five numbers to call within the hour where I can now get a hold of somebody. So she's doing this in the background for me. I pay her by the hour and she works from her house.

Jim: I have never heard of that before, and that's brilliant! You've basically got somebody making calls to find out if somebody is there and answering their phone, and therefore you then know to call that person very soon, because they'll most likely answer the phone when you call.

Mike: Absolutely, so it's more efficient.

Jim: That's brilliant! Wow, I love that. That's great!

Mike: I thought I'd share that with you.

Jim: Hey, you're always about increasing efficiency. Having done this a long time myself, it's not too often that I hear a new idea that I've never heard of before, and this is great. I love it! So for anybody who's calling people, particularly at home where they're answering their phones directly, that would be phenomenal if you want to go in that direction. You could maybe even have a virtual assistant do that for you. That's brilliant.

When you're prospecting someone, what is the goal that you want to accomplish on the prospecting call?

Mike: Get an appointment. That's the #1 and only goal, just to set an appointment. There's no other reason to be calling. I look at it as a numbers game, but the numbers really aren't as important as setting an appointment. I could call three people in four hours, and if I got one appointment I'd be happy. Again, I have to do the numbers in order for it to average out, but it's all about setting an appointment, Jim.

Jim: So you want to meet with the person face-to-face, because you know that's crucial towards getting them to remember you, to differentiate you from the competition, so that they're going to want to work with you ahead of everyone else.

Mike: Absolutely.

Jim: That's great, and so few people focus in on that. I think it's good that you really just want to make sure that you're meeting with the people that you want to do business with.

I remember when I first started in commercial real estate brokerage myself over 30 years ago, the guy who was my manager at the time said the same thing. You want to do whatever you can to meet with somebody, because the relationship then moves to the next level after you've met with them, and there's a certain feeling of a bond, or that you now know each other better.

That can't happen just from making a phone call.

Mike: And when you're there, the opportunity is so much greater to get a contract signed. It's there. If they're interested in what you have to say and there's a motivation...of course I don't go on these appointments unless I sense there's motivation. I'm not going to just be a professional visitor.

Jim: There you go. It's important that you have a good sense of knowing when something could lead to more business for you.

Mike: Absolutely. Oh yes.

Jim: When you get started doing your prospecting early first thing in the morning, it's tougher to get sucked into the drama of all these other things that come up that keep telling you, "No, no, Mike, you've got to do this instead, and make your calls later on in the day." That's important.

So out of every 10 phone calls you make, how many live conversations are you actually having with prospects?

Mike: Are you talking about just dials?

Jim: Yes. When you're dialing, how many times are you actually speaking to a live person on the other end, versus having to leave a voicemail message for them?

Mike: I would say I have to dial 10 to get 2 live on the telephone with me on the average.

Jim: That percentage is probably a little bit higher because you've got the other person calling to find out if people are answering their phone.

Mike: Oh yes, that helps with a little more leverage.

Jim: I really love that idea.

So when you're calling somebody and you actually get transferred into voicemail, do you leave a message for the person?

Mike: I do. Not all the time, but I do. And if I feel that it's something that could possibly get their interest and attention, I would certainly do that. I've gotten results out of that. The other thing that I do is I use an unrestricted line that I'm calling out on, so sometimes when I call there's nobody there, but they'll call back because my name and my phone number are visible to them, and that has worked out well for me.

Every once in a while, about an hour later I'm hearing my phone ring. Then all of a sudden I've got their attention. So every once in a while I don't leave a message and they still call back.

Jim: Have you got any recommendations for how brokers can make sure that they get their prospecting done, instead of blowing it off and getting distracted by other things?

Mike: I think first of all they need to understand how valuable prospecting is. One of the things that I do at the end of the year is look and see the source of my business and the value of the time that I'm spending. I get a lot of business from past clients, because over the years I've represented so many people, but I look at some of the new business I've generated, and half of my business could be from just prospecting, so you've got to really put a value to it. I think that's really #1.

Also, be able to put that time in as a very valuable part of your week and day. You've got to segment it and put that into your schedule. There are so many distractions. We get distractions because somebody's calling us on our cell phone, or somebody rushes into your office and says, "So and so's got to speak to you now!", and so forth.

I put everything on hold for my prospecting because I know that those hours are sacred. That is time to generate real dollars. All these other interruptions are just very weak possibilities of something that can't wait. Most of them really can wait.

Jim: Brokers, when they're not doing their prospecting can be thinking, "Oh, it's really important and every broker needs to prospect," but then when you're in the heat of battle with all these other things crying out for your attention, it's another story. "You've got to get me done now. You can't do your prospecting now". These are the kinds of things that just come at you. I think oftentimes what's going on subconsciously is the fear of the rejection is kicking in, and the brokers are buying into it. It's human nature in many ways, and that's why very few people, relatively speaking, ever become commercial real estate brokers.

Mike: These are all basically excuses, and I think if we really are honest with ourselves, we really need to take a closer look. I can make excuses all the time. Believe me, I could write you a book on it, but it's about making money in our business. The good news is there's very little competition to deal with out there when times get tough, so we have an opportunity to swing the bat a lot more often and hit home runs, when we're just doing the things that are really going to pay off.

What else are we going to do? Sit in the office and wait? Tell me. What else are we going to do?

Jim: Well, paper shuffling, time on the internet, this feeling that I'm really "busy, busy, busy", but I'm not really being productive. You can delude yourself into confusing being "busy" for being productive. We can all be busy on minutiae, and on other things like that.

But if you're not out there hustling business and contacting people that you hope you can do business with, you're basically doing follow-up, which is necessary on transactions, but you're not developing more new business when you're doing follow-up, and you've got to do both of these activities together. You've got to do your follow-up, and you've got to keep your prospecting going on, because the prospecting is what provides the leads for the deals you'll be closing down the road in the future.

Mike: We have to remember that we're filling our pipeline every day. It's got to be filled every day. If we just want to do a couple of deals, that's not a problem. But if we want to reach goals in excess of what we did last year, let's say that we want to produce twice what we did last year, then we have to really be filling that pipeline every single day to make sure that there's always business coming in after the next deal closes.

Jim: So many brokers prospect until they get busy with leads, and then they drop out their prospecting, or reduce it substantially while they're busy following up on the leads that they've generated. But this is going to lead to inconsistent production, holes in your pipeline, and all sorts of things that you don't want to be involved in. But you can kind of lose sight of that in the moment when you're busy following up on all the deals that are on your lap, and you stop doing your prospecting.

Mike: Absolutely. Most of the stuff that we do can wait until the afternoon. That's why it's important to do your prospecting early. Get it out of the way, and then I feel so good after 1:00 p.m. because I know I've done the most important activity of my day. That's such a great feeling!

Jim: Yes, and you mentioned that you go to the gym early in the morning, too. That's one of the reasons for going to the gym early in the morning, because you get it done, you get it out of the way, and you don't have the ability to run the same excuses that you can at 6:00 p.m., as to why you can't go to the gym now at the end of the day. But you can still run the excuses when the alarm goes off in the morning as to why you shouldn't be getting up and going to the gym! [laughing]

Mike: Absolutely. [laughing]

Jim: You mentioned a couple of minutes ago about how you could write a book on excuses, and I'm sitting here thinking, "No wonder you said what you did about the things that you listen to at the gym in the morning." You probably don't want to make a recording with all these excuses to listen to in the gym, right? [laughing] That would take you down a completely different path to begin the day!

I heard Woody Allen say once that he bought the greatest tape recorder in the world. He said he talks into it and it just keeps saying, "I know, I know."

Talking about prospecting and getting it done consistently, this is so important for a number of different reasons. Two of the reasons you want to keep getting your prospecting done, no matter how busy you are, are 1) It will allow you to elevate the quality of the clients you're working with, and 2) It will allow you to increase the average commission you're earning per transaction, and here's why:

When you keep doing your prospecting, you're developing more and more leads, and you're going, "Wait a second, I can't work on all of these leads," so you've got to let go of the more marginal ones and/or hand them off to another broker who can work on them instead, and you can maybe even earn a referral fee for this, too.

Therefore, now you're only working on better and better commission opportunities, and you're only working with people who are going to be more loyal to you, because you're selecting the cream of the crop from these leads you've now generated. In addition, you're going to earn more money per transaction, because you're choosing the higher-commission leads to work with, and you're now discarding the lower-commission opportunities.

But if you stop doing your prospecting because you've already been generating leads, you'll never see these higher-commission opportunities, and they'll be going to your competitors instead, because your competitors will be prospecting these people.

So many commercial brokers feel that they need to work on every single lead that they uncover. But this can lead to feeling overwhelmed, and it can cause the broker to stop prospecting, too. So you need to recognize that it's important to prospect continually, then work on the best, higher-commission-opportunity leads, and discard the more marginal leads that you were working on previously.

Mike: That's a really good point there, Jim. It reminds me of prioritizing my day. When I broke this down years ago I really got it. There are really five activities that I found myself doing that really would generate income. It was prospecting, lead follow-up, setting appointments, and negotiating contracts. Then the last one was administrative work. So I gave 80% to the first four, and then 20% to administrative work.

Every day I looked to see, "Where did my time go?" If it wasn't into lead generation and prospecting, then I really wasn't taking care of business. I was just doing work that I shouldn't be doing.

Jim: I completely agree with you, Mike.

So now what we're going to do is segue into my presentation directly to the audience. As I mentioned earlier, there are certain things around prospecting that I want to make sure to communicate to everyone tonight, so I'm going to be talking to everyone directly here for about 20 minutes. Then after I'm done, we'll return again to my interview with Mike.

So let's begin by talking about the importance of having your database in great shape so you have all the information you want on every single prospect you want to do business with. Because if you're calling people when doing your telephone prospecting, or you're mailing or emailing to them, if there are important people who are not in your database, how do they even know that you exist? They may see your signs around town, but that's about it.

Everybody that you want to do business with, you want to have in your database so you can contact them with your prospecting calls, or send mail or email to them about what's going on in your territory. But if they're not in your database and they're in your competitors' databases, your competitors can then contact them about doing business with them, but you can't.

With this in mind, here are some resources and services that you can utilize to improve your database and find more prospects, in addition to finding their contact information, too. These are basically resources that I know are very valid for here in the United States. So if you're outside the country these may or may not work for you, and in addition, I've got one resource for people in Canada that I'll give to you in just a couple of minutes. Keep in mind, though, that these resources can always be replaced by new and better companies and services at any given moment in time, but these resources are both good and valid for this exact moment in time.

A good website and service for commercial agents is located at www.ProspectNow.com. Steve Wayne is the President of that company, he's a former Marcus & Millichap agent, and they've got information on millions of commercial property owners here in the U.S., and information on millions of tenants and businesses, too. In addition, they've got the phone numbers for 60% or more of all of the property owners in their database.

Again, that's www.ProspectNow.com for all of that information. It's a great service, especially if you're missing information in your database and you want to find the right decision makers.

In addition, another company that provides services similar to Prospect Now is Reonomy, which is located at www.Reonomy.com.

Also here in the United States there's www.LexisNexis.com. You can get property ownership information here, property owner contact information, and you can find out who the individuals are behind the partnerships, the corporations, or the LLCs that own the property.

They may still be doing this, but I know several years ago you actually had to pass a security check to have them allow you to utilize their information, because it's so sensitive, and they've got so much detailed information on people that they want to make sure that the people they're giving access to the information are completely above-board and good people.

There's a broker who I've coached who had another broker in his office say, "I wish I could find this one property owner's phone number, but I can't." So the broker that I coach, who was using LexisNexis said, "Let me go to work on this for you." Then he told me, "Jim, I found the owner's phone number within five minutes, but I didn't tell the broker about it for two days, because I knew if I gave it to him in just five minutes he'd be all over me, asking me how I did it. He competes with me in my territory in some ways, so I didn't want to tell him about this service. But I wanted to help him out at the same time, too."

This is a solid service for getting the kind of information that you want on property owners, along with getting their contact information.

In addition, many brokers now like the service located at www.TLO.com, a service I'm told that can really help you to uncover both the phone numbers and specific information on the property owners and the principals that you really want to be doing business with.

Then if you're in the retail sector, there's www.PlainVanillaShell.com that's a good resource. If you're working with retail people and retail tenants, they've got a retail directory you can get access to with ongoing information on more than 5,000 retail chains that are actively expanding into additional locations. They have news there on what's going on with major players within the retail industry, too.

In Canada, if you're interested in information on property owners and property ownership, let me give you one website that's been recommended to me by different commercial brokers operating within Canada, and that website is located at www.RealNet.ca.

OK. Now let's talk about prospecting. The most important part of prospecting is you getting it done every single week, as so many brokers just don't get their prospecting done to the level that they know they should be. In order to make this happen, I recommend that you schedule your prospecting time in advance every single week. Block it out in your contact management software program, and then hold that time sacred. You want to treat it like it's a listing presentation appointment with an owner, in order to obtain a multimillion-dollar listing.

For example, you wouldn't normally call an owner to cancel a listing appointment at the last minute because something else has come up, would you? So don't do this with your prospecting time either.

I always recommend that if you've got prospecting time scheduled and you're thinking, "You know, I really need to do these other things instead, so I can't really get my prospecting done today," ask yourself, "If I had an appointment for a three or four million-dollar listing presentation right now, would I call the owner up and say, 'I'm sorry, I can't make the presentation. These other things have come up and they're now more important.'"

If your answer to that question is "No," then just get your prospecting done with no excuses, because you definitely do have the time.

Also ask yourself the question, "If I were to prospect 10-12 hours every single week for the next year, what kind of results do I think I'd be producing in my commercial real estate brokerage business?" And if you like your answer to that question, just get your prospecting done with no excuses.

Sometimes when I speak in front of commercial real estate brokerage audiences, I may be scheduled to speak for anywhere between one to three hours. So very early in the presentation I might ask that exact same question to the audience. Then the people in the audience will tell me that prospecting 10-12 hours a week every single week for the next year would literally explode their brokerage business, increasing their commissions by anywhere between 30% and 200%.

Then jokingly I say, "OK, great! My work is done here. I don't really need to say anything more to you. You've been a great audience, and I look forward to seeing you again the next time." Then people begin smiling and laughing, as I'm still within the very first five minutes of my presentation to them, but what I've just said is the truth. If you get only one activity accomplished, get your prospecting done every single week with no excuses, and watch how much better your results start getting.

I always believe it's best to get your prospecting done first thing in the morning. Get it done before lunch, because if you try to do it in the afternoon, and you schedule it for let's say between 1:00 p.m. and 4:00 p.m., when 1:00

p.m. comes around you might say, "Uh-oh, I've got all of these other things I need to get done by 5:00 p.m., so I can't get my prospecting done today."

Does this sound familiar to you?

If you get your prospecting done by 11:00 a.m. or noon, now you've got the entire rest of the day to get everything done that needs to be done by 5:00 p.m. or 6:00 p.m. So when you do your prospecting in the morning, it gives you fewer excuses as to why you don't have the time to get it done, because you've still got half the day left after you've gotten your prospecting done.

Several years ago I interviewed a solid Cushman & Wakefield broker on one of my teleconferences. He's a very successful broker who works with large national companies as his clients, and he mentioned something he does that's helped him tremendously in dealing with the rejection that we all face when prospecting. He said he likes to pretend that he's actually playing the role of someone else doing the prospecting, instead of it being himself who's the one doing the prospecting.

It's similar to playing a character in a movie. You're a character who's playing the role of someone doing telephone prospecting, so that when you get rejected, it's not like they're rejecting you personally, they're rejecting your character instead.

He said for him this really softens the blow when people get upset and slam down the phone on him, so I wanted to mention this in case this is something you'd like to try that you believe could make your prospecting even more enjoyable.

As in the movie, the actor playing the prospecting character isn't going to take it personally whenever they get rejected, and the better you can become at feeling you're playing a prospecting character, too, maybe even someone who's highly driven, charismatic, confident, and who lets rejection just bounce right off of them, the more successful you'll become at doing your prospecting, and the more easily you'll get your prospecting done, too.

So it's not you that they're rejecting, it's now your character. Then at the end of your prospecting session, you step out of your character, and step back into being yourself.

OK. Now let's talk about some options for scripting when you're doing your prospecting. Let's first talk about the situation when you're talking with and trying to get past the gatekeeper, or the receptionist, when you're calling your prospects on the telephone. These people are oftentimes trained to screen out salespeople and put them into voicemail, according to the criteria that the decision maker has given them.

If you know the decision maker's name, just ask for them directly. For example, let's say the decision maker is John Robinson. You call the company on the telephone, the receptionist answers, and you can then say, "John Robinson, please." You might even consider, if you feel OK with it, asking for the person by their first name only, because this will sound more to the gatekeeper like you may already know John personally, and that you already have a relationship with him. So instead of asking for John Robinson you could just say, "John, please," when the receptionist answers the telephone. I used to do this myself with my prospecting, too, when I was a full-time industrial broker. This can sometimes help to at least elevate you to the level where the receptionist may be thinking, "Oh, he must know my boss, so I should be forwarding this call directly onto my boss."

If the gatekeeper asks you what the call is regarding, your response can depend on whether you're calling an owner, or a tenant. For example, your goal in this situation in telling the gatekeeper what the call is about is to get the decision maker interested in getting on the phone and talking with you, when the gatekeeper tells the decision maker what the call is regarding.

So if you're calling someone who's a tenant you could say, "I have some office space available at an unbelievably low rate, and I want to talk to John about it." So therefore you'll want to have this information available to talk to the principal about whenever they come onto the call one-on-one with you.

Keep in mind when you're talking through the gatekeeper, there's going to be a certain amount of filtering going on with how they communicate what you've said to them when they tell it to the decision maker. You'll want to be brief, to the point, and sound exciting with what you're communicating to the gatekeeper, because if you're lengthy and wordy, it's most likely not going to sound nearly as exciting when they're relaying that information to the decision maker, because they'll be lengthy and wordy, too, when they're communicating the information themselves.

You just want to make sure that you sound exciting, and that you make your communication short and sweet, so that they can communicate this short and sweet message with excitement to the decision maker.

If you're calling a property owner, and the gatekeeper asks you what the call is regarding, you could say, "I've got a building for sale near one of his properties," or "I've got a great investment for sale near one of his properties," because many investors are curious about what's going on near their own properties, and hearing about a property coming onto the market near one of theirs could be just the right hook to get them interested in getting on the phone and talking with you.

But let's face it, many times you're going to be leaving voicemail messages for the decision maker, and we'll get into how to best do that in just a couple of minutes.

When you get through live to the decision maker, here are some ideas on what you can say when beginning your conversation. What you say the moment you first get connected live with the decision maker is extremely important, because your goal with the first words that come out of your mouth is to get the decision maker interested in staying on the phone and engaging in a live conversation with you.

Yes, I know you'd like to communicate information and ask them questions, but first of all you want to get the decision maker interested in talking with you, as this makes the rest of the conversation flow much easier, and it has them feeling that they want to stay on the telephone longer with you.

So you want to open up the conversation right away by offering them something they may be interested in. For example, for a decision maker who's a tenant, similar to what we said before you could begin the conversation with, "I've got some office space available near you at an unbelievably low rate, and I want to know if this is something you could be interested in."

Now keep in mind, you just need to do some research ahead of time and find the office space that's available at an unbelievably low rate. It could even be a sublease where the sublessor is extremely motivated to just find someone to move in and occupy the space, and begin paying them some rent. The space doesn't need to be 'Class A' space either, as your goal is to get the decision maker to begin engaging in a conversation with you, and have them begin asking you questions.

So in a short period of time during your conversation, you may find that the space isn't really what the decision maker is looking for, and you can then ask them, "So what is it that you ARE looking for?"

They may be looking for something, or they may just be curious as to what's going on in the marketplace. But either way, once they've begun talking with you, this makes it easier for you to then stay on the phone longer with them. Then it becomes easier to ask them for information like when their lease is expiring.

Or if your company offers lease audits or lease analysis as part of your services you could say, "We've found that 54% of the tenants in your area have been overpaying their landlords and they're not even aware of it. Would you like to find out if you've been overpaying your landlord?" Then you would move towards discussing what's involved in you doing a lease audit or a lease analysis for them, and then move towards scheduling a time to meet with them.

If you're calling a decision maker who's a property owner, you could begin the conversation with, "There's a building on the market near yours that I think will give you a great idea of what your building is worth in today's market. Would you be interested in hearing about this?" Again, many owners are usually curious to learn about what's been happening with the other buildings near their own, especially if it will help them to understand the current value of their own building.

When you ask opening questions like these to owners and tenants when you're prospecting them, when they tell you they're interested in hearing the information that you're offering them, they've now opened the door for you to engage in a one-on-one conversation with them. They're basically inviting you in saying, "Yes, please tell me about the information that you've got. I'd like to know more about it."

Because you're now telling them something that they want to know about, they're more likely to let you ask them more questions about their own property afterwards...questions like when their lease is expiring, or questions about their current situation and their plans with their property, or about whether or not they're interested in selling. This is all because of the law of reciprocity: **When you do something nice for someone, they'll feel like they want to reciprocate and do something nice for you, too.**

It's similar to the old saying, "There's no such thing as a free lunch". When you take somebody out to lunch, or to a nice meal and you spend money on them, they'll feel like they want to give something back to you when they have the opportunity, and the most logical way to give back to you is by giving you business whenever they have their next commercial real estate requirement. This is why taking people to lunch, giving them gifts, and socializing with them can be extremely powerful. When you've done things like this on an ongoing basis for your people, this makes it very difficult for them to ever think about working with one of your competitors instead.

Let's now talk about leaving a voicemail message that gets the decision maker more interested in calling you back. The great thing about leaving a voicemail message for someone is that they get to hear exactly what you're telling them with the exact same excitement and the exact same tone of voice that you're telling it to them in, without anything being filtered out by the gatekeeper.

So when leaving voicemail messages for owners or tenants, you might consider saying something similar to the following. "Steve, I have some industrial space available near you at an unbelievably low rate per square foot, and I want to know if this is something you may be interested in." Or "Cheryl, a building has just come on the market near yours that I think will give you an excellent idea of what your property is worth right now in today's market. Would you be interested in hearing about it?"

Or to cover more bases, if you don't know what exactly they may be interested in, you could say something like, "Dan, I've got two buildings available in your area; one I feel is an outstanding investment opportunity that you could buy, and the other represents the lowest lease rate per square foot that I've seen in today's market."

In addition, here's one more possibility. You could leave a message saying, "Bob, I've just put together a comps report showing you what all the buildings in your area have sold and leased for over the past six months. I've only got three of these reports left, so if you want one of them call me now and I'll make sure that you get one."

There's a good chance that anyone who's looking to buy, sell, or lease will want to get their hands on this report to better understand what's going on right now in the market, so your offer in your voicemail message may inspire them to pick up the phone, call you, and tell you to get them a copy of the report. Then when you're talking to them on the phone and you're getting their information so you can get them a copy of the report, you can simply ask them, "Just out of curiosity, do you plan on buying, selling, or leasing in the near future?"

In all of these situations that I've mentioned, it's about doing what you can to catch their attention with something they might be interested in, and communicating this with excitement in your voice to get them curious enough to call you back.

If you think you've got something even better than this that you can utilize to catch their attention and interest with, write a script with this on your own and then utilize the script when you're doing your prospecting.

The last thing you ever want to do is leave a boring voicemail message and say something like, "Hi, this is Bill, and I'm calling to see if you have any real estate needs." There's really no reason for them to call you back, because they're hearing this from all of the other brokers, too. You've basically just differentiated yourself like a box of cereal on the shelf in the supermarket, that's all white in color, except for just having one blue stripe around it.

So instead, you want to really differentiate yourself and dangle a carrot in front of them with something they may really want to bite on if they're interested in buying, selling, or leasing. When you're fishing, you don't expect the fish to come up and bite on your fishing hook just because you want to catch a fish. You determine, "What will they be biting on?", and then you put that on the hook.

Prospecting, metaphorically speaking, can be very similar to this.

With that being said, now it's time to segue back into my interview with our special guest, Mike Monteleone, CCIM. Mike, are you there?

Mike: Yes, Jim. I've been taking some notes. I've been prospecting for many years in our industry, and I'm always learning. You had some really great things to say in there!

Jim: Thanks for the kind words, Mike. If I'm saying some things that even you can learn from, being the great prospector that you are, then I'm definitely doing good.

Mike: Absolutely!

Jim: So in continuing on with our interview, we've been talking about prospecting, and prospecting is just one part of the equation for closing more business. The second part of the equation, generally speaking, is closing people successfully on working with you exclusively, which involves having solid presentation skills. Once you have exclusive representation agreements in place, be they with owners, buyers, or lessees, you now have a great chance of making some money. You still need to be able to negotiate successfully, but now you're the only broker who can close a transaction with the client for their current commercial real estate need.

With this in mind, how important do you think having solid presentation skills is within our industry?

Mike: I think presentation skills are really critical. It's really important to try to get in rapport quickly over the telephone. The personality styles are really important for us to understand. In essence, I put it into four categories. You have the amiable, the analytical, the expressive, and the drivers, and if we can understand who they are when they immediately answer the phone, you've got to quickly move yourself in that direction to get the rapport going. It's something that I learned years ago with neurolinguistic training, and it's helped me a lot, Jim.

Jim: You're one of the few people I can talk to who understands Neurolinguistic Programming.

Mike: We want to mimic their rate of speech and even their accents sometimes. We try to get into the flow so people feel comfortable talking to you, so you're not just another telemarketer.

Jim: And actually, since you brought that up, I've got a book that I want to recommend to everybody. Long-time members in my program will recognize it because I've been recommending it for a while, but we've got a lot of new people that have come into the program recently.

It's called *Unlimited Selling Power: How to Master Hypnotic Selling Skills*, and the authors are Donald Moine and Kenneth Lloyd. This is a book that does a great job for people who have not really been exposed much to knowing how to build great rapport, and how to phrase something in a question to someone that actually moves them closer to closing the sale. Many times salespeople say things that actually repel people away from working with them, and this book discusses this and gives you examples of this.

They actually came out with a second book with an almost identical title. You want to get the book that has the subtitle, "How to Master Hypnotic Selling Skills." When you listen to what's in the book you'll find yourself saying, "Oh wow, if I said that in this situation instead of what I've normally been saying, I recognize that this will now work much better for me in brokerage."

I just wanted to mention that since you brought this subject up, Mike. I think it's a great book for people to learn more about how to be more effective with their language when they're talking to the people they want to do business with.

Mike: And another point, too, and this is really hard because our egos get in the way of this one, is to record your telephone conversations, then you'll really get a chance to see how well you're doing, or how much you need to still improve on using your scripts. I did that for probably six months and I really learned a lot about why I was not getting appointments, why people were hanging up the phone on me, and it's just really a great learning experience.

My ego got in the way so many times. I'd say, "Oh, I already know how to do that. That's their problem. They're having a bad day," and so forth, and I was blaming them. But I was really the one responsible. It all fits into what you've mentioned, and that book should be a great one.

Jim: Since you mentioned recording, something else that I recommend to brokers is recording their listing presentation on video, too. Sit in an office-type of environment with somebody else role playing along with you as the decision maker that you want to obtain a listing from, and then record the entire presentation. Then leave the camera running at the end of the presentation, and ask the person for their feedback and input on how you did.

Get all of that recorded, and then watch it back at some point, and you'll start to notice things as Mike just mentioned. You'll notice things, and then you'll say something like, "Wow, I could really improve on this. I wasn't even aware that I was doing this!" So this can be extremely powerful to improve your presentation skills, take them to the next level, and then close even more business.

If you up your presentation abilities so you close more business, now you're going to be closing more business and earning more commissions from the exact same number of leads you were previously generating. For example, let's say after every listing presentation maybe 50% of the time you're the broker who ends up getting the listing, as opposed to it being someone else.

If you improve your listing presentation skills and you're able to increase that closing percentage from 50% up to 60%, so that you're now closing just one more person out of every 10 that you deliver your listing presentation to, that's a difference of 20% in your income, in going from 50% up to 60%! That 10% differential divided by the original 50% means that you're now landing 20% more listings from your newer, more improved presentations. So I highly recommend that you record your presentations, and watch them back and learn from them.

Do you think that's a good idea, Mike?

Mike: Oh, absolutely.

Jim: You're already recording your telephone presentations, and very few people would even do that, so I know you're constantly trying to improve your skills in any way that you can, and that's great.

When the market gets tough, what do you think will differentiate the top-producing brokers from everyone else?

Mike: First of all, mindset. You've got to work on mindset all the time, because for those that are optimistic and have good energy, people will want to deal with you. You don't want to be doom and gloom when you're talking to people. You have to be the person that has the answers, that has solutions, that can get the job done, so that's #1.

Also, you have to have a good work ethic. They have to sense that you're well-organized, you're disciplined, you're aggressive, etcetera. Some people say, "It's all luck." Well, I define L.U.C.K. as Labor Under Correct Knowledge. You've got to have the knowledge and you have to put the time in and work hard. People acknowledge that. Showing up on time, doing what you say you're going to do, your work habits, the mental toughness, the mindset, all of that has a lot to do with clients choosing you over the competition.

Jim: You talked about luck and working hard. I remember there's a quote that I've heard many times over the years, and I don't remember who's the original source of it, but it's "The harder I work, the luckier I get."

Mike: There you go! My acronym is that W.O.R.K. is defined as Warranted Organized Relentless Kickass effort.

Jim: That's great! Just saying that alone can kind of get you excited and pumped up.

Mike: No kidding!

Jim: You talked about mastering one's mindset, and I know there are different things you do, and listening to the recordings in the morning is just one part of that. Do you have any other insights in terms of what brokers can do to master that mindset and live in a state of expectancy, in being certain that you're always going to uncover another great opportunity?

Mike: First of all, you can't take all the news that we hear seriously, because in essence that's not going to make a difference in your day. Because if you do the right things every day you're going to get the results. So we don't want to be at the effect of negative news, and there's negative news coming at us all day long as we know.

The mindset to develop this comes from reading good positive books, listening to great audio recordings, and getting your mind focused on making things happen, being optimistic, setting big goals, and reading your goals every day. That helps me a lot. That's why I do about 30 minutes on my goals every day. I just listen to everything that I want to accomplish this year, and then I do my long-term goals. So I have a separate section for my long-term goals.

Then the other thing is to really have a "what for." Why am I doing all of this? Have a big enough dream or goal to achieve, so that you really get excited about it.

Jim: Yes, it's like the goals are one thing, but when you're really clear on why you want it, why it's important, and you know how you're going to feel when you manifest that goal, that's really the engine that will totally drive and propel you towards accomplishing the goal.

We've got people here listening to us that are in different places in their careers, experiencing different levels of success. But I know that especially for brokers who have been around, when times get tough there can be a feeling of, "Oh my gosh, I'm working so hard. The results aren't coming anywhere near like they used to be," and there's a certain feeling of burn-out and frustration that the game plan they're using just isn't working anymore. So when this hits, they can kind of feel like they're running low on energy, and like they're continually bumping their head into a wall.

What do you recommend to a broker who's feeling like that?

Mike: Obviously I've been there several times myself. You have to kind of step back and really analyze your business and the things you're doing, and the time you're spending, and also evaluate the ways that you're doing it. A good coach can really take a look at this objectively to kind of help move you in the right direction. Just one or two thoughts or ideas from a good coach can change your business dramatically.

I remember a gal that used to do nothing but apartments for me. She worked for me and she was a very aggressive gal, she really wanted to become successful, and she kept calling apartment owners.

She'd come back week after week saying, "Mike, it's just not happening, it's just not happening. Nobody wants to sell. I'm calling these people and they've already sold their building," and I said, "Well, what does that tell you?"

She said, "What do you mean?"

I said, "If they're selling their property, there are obviously transactions going on. If you get to the right one at the right time, you're going to be the one to sell their building."

That totally shifted her thinking. The next week we had a 20-unit building listed, and this was all because she had changed her mindset.

So just one or two little things could change the direction of your business, but we have to be open enough to get some coaching and some direction. We also have to just look at our own activities and realize that sometimes we just have to change what we're doing, and do it fast enough so that it doesn't impact us negatively.

Jim: You're right, Mike. A good coach can make a tremendous difference, and even though my own business is coaching commercial real estate brokers, I've got coaches with different areas of expertise that coach me in different areas within my business, too. I just think this is hugely important, and I know you've been a big fan and proponent of coaching for many, many years now, too.

Also, for those people who may be bumping their heads against the wall, take a step back sometime. Take a day or two off and get away from not seeing the forest for the trees, and do some creative thinking, and some writing about implementing good, new ideas into your business.

A process that I've recommended to people for years now is to go someplace quiet, maybe even outdoors, and have a stack of index cards along with you, and just sit there for an hour or two, writing down every single idea you can think of that could grow your business. Nowadays there are index card apps that will allow you to do this electronically, so just choose the approach that's best for you.

Write down one idea per index card, and then move onto the next clean index card to write down your next idea.

Then when you're done, go back to work, but take some time soon to go through those cards and say, "What are the top 3-5 ideas in here that would make the greatest positive difference in my business if I implemented them?" You can always implement more of the ideas that you've written down, but usually there will be 3-5 ideas that will make the greatest difference, and those are the ones you'll want to begin implementing immediately.

That creative thinking can be hugely important, and writing down the ideas on each individual index card, or in an index card app, will preserve them there for you. You can then go back and look at them and decide which ones you'll want to begin capitalizing on.

Mike: And also, when the market is more difficult, you'll have to put in the extra time and effort. In those kinds of markets, I find myself working twice as hard as I would like to be working to make a good living. It's not something I look forward to having to do, but my goals are such that I do it and I make sure that I enjoy doing it, because I have a big enough picture of the "what for" in front of me, and I know what I want to accomplish during the year.

Jim: With somebody with your decades of experience, prospecting 20 hours a week in more difficult times really makes a statement for how much everybody should really be prospecting, because you know you've got to do it in that kind of economy to develop the leads for the business that you want to close.

You mentioned earlier about not paying attention to the negativity and the bad news. You reminded me of something again from Woody Allen that I mention from time-to-time. Woody Allen used to have a bit that he'd use when he was closing his stand-up comedy routines way back when. He'd say, "In summing up, I wish I had some sort of positive message to leave you all with. Would you take instead maybe...two negative messages?" [laughing] It's so perfect within his character basically, the old idea from elementary school that two negatives make a positive when you're multiplying.

I know you've managed a lot of agents during your real estate career. We've got people listening who are brokers acting as independent contractors on their own, and people who have teams. In addition, we've also got people listening who are managers and/or owners of their own brokerage companies. With this in mind, what recommendations do you have for anyone who may be listening who's currently managing agents, on how they can manage their own agents more effectively?

Mike: Well, this is for both types of people. As you know, I had my own company for several years and I remember explicitly with my investment manager, we designed a weekly call night. We made it fun. You can't make it mandatory, but we sure made it important, and we did get a good turnout.

As I monitored the results over the next three or four months, everybody was doing business. It was just an exciting thing. So one of the things that we started to do after that when we saw that it really worked was to have weekly accountability meetings with our individual agents.

The agent should look forward to this. It's something that will only benefit you in your production by looking at it from a different point of view, and having somebody there holding you accountable to your promises and your goals. What else is there? We're in business to make money, so why not have the support to make it happen?

So we did weekly accountability meetings, and we also did monthly reviews. We really were able to make sure that every agent that was committed to really do well, that they were on track. So we got them on track.

At this time especially, I would highly recommend that you take a personal interest in sitting down with each agent, going over their goals, going over their activities, going over their results, and that's a good time to be coaching on certain things that you see are missing, or that should be added or increased.

Then just work with them on a weekly basis in private. I looked forward to it. When I was being coached early on in my career, if one or two things came out of that meeting I was like, "Oh, that's what I need to do." I needed to know how to close, so my manager would say, "Try this particular approach," and I closed deals, so it was worth it.

Let's get our egos out of the way, and the manager needs to not be fearful of making a request, because it's for everyone's benefit.

Jim: Something that I want to add to that also...for managers, a real simple way to do something to help create more accountability, is you could just for example every Friday have all your agents turn in a sheet of paper telling you how many prospecting calls they've made, or how many hours they've prospected, which as a manager will give you some insight into any problem situations where a broker's been off-track from prospecting for a while.

But not only that, when the agent looks at this, it can oftentimes serve as a kick in their own butt to say, "Wow, if I only did two hours of prospecting each week for the last two weeks, I've really got to get moving!" Sometimes when you're filling out that form on Friday, you can just say, "I'm sick and tired of looking at these low numbers. I've got to ratchet it up to 10-12 hours a week." Whereas without that accountability within the process of filling out the form, the agent can continue on feeling busy without getting their prospecting done, and they can still not really realize that they're off-track a ton within their own business.

Mike: Jim, I want to just add something, too, because my son and I are accountable to each other every day. At the end of the day he knows how many past clients I need to contact every day. I have a minimum of six past clients that I have to talk to, and he has a minimum of five.

So we have a little deal, that if we don't hit our numbers he's got to pay me $20.00, or I pay him $20.00 if I don't at least get to my past clients, and I haven't missed a day, and neither has he. Just that little accountability factor means a lot.

Every day at the end of the day he emails me his numbers...every day, not every week, and at the end of the week he gives me a tally of the total. I sit down with him once a week and we go over his plan, his goals, and then also his objectives, and also what we need to do in order to adjust his schedule.

So it's important I think to have an accountability partner, and any agent can do that in your office, or even have your manager for that matter just work with you, and you can do it every day. Believe me, you'll get more done, you'll get better results, and the accountability is very empowering.

Jim: Sometimes with my one-on-one coaching clients, if they haven't been getting their prospecting done I'll tell them to pick a charity that they'd like to donate money to, and then in the next week between our calls if they don't get all their prospecting calls done, then they have to cut a check for a specific amount to that charity. Sometimes, right away, they get the message and they start getting their prospecting done, and sometimes it takes a few weeks before they finally go, "Alright, I don't want to cut a check again next week, so I'd better make these calls!" [laughing]

We have a question from Catherine. Catherine, please go ahead with your question.

Catherine: Hi guys. Mike, you mentioned on the call that you spend 80% of your time setting appointments, prospecting, doing lead generation, and what was the fourth item that you said?

Mike: Negotiating contracts.

Catherine: Great.

Jim: Did that answer your question?

Catherine: That did. Thank you.

Jim: Thanks, Catherine. The next question comes from Len. Len please state your question.

Len: Thanks, Jim. Both of you have given me some great ideas for getting my prospecting done! My question is, for someone who's an industrial broker, do you recommend prospecting people on the phone, or prospecting them by walking into their place of business?

Jim: Let me take a run at this first, Mike, and then I'll turn it over to you to see if you've got something you want to add to it.

First of all, I would tend to gravitate towards whatever you feel you would enjoy doing the most, because if you feel you'd love or enjoy one more than the other, and you don't particularly care for the other approach, I would tend to gravitate towards doing the one that you enjoy, because that will probably help you to get more prospecting done.

But keep in mind with industrial properties, when you're calling people on the phone you have the ability to call either the tenants who are occupying the building, or the owners, wherever the owners may be located.

However, when you're knocking on doors and walking in on people located in industrial properties, the majority of the time you'll be talking to tenants who are leasing the building, because the owners will be located someplace else. The only exception will be when you're talking to owner/users, who own the building they're located in.

So if you want to focus on getting listings, you'll definitely want to be calling owners on the telephone also.

When you're doing telephone prospecting, you can call more people per hour than you can contact when you're canvassing and walking in on people. But in my opinion, when you're sitting in someone's office waiting to see them, you've got a higher probability of talking to them. However, this probability then diminishes, generally speaking, the larger the building is that you're walking in on, and the more corporate that the culture is within the building.

Mike, do you have anything you'd like to add to that?

Mike: I totally agree. I think that on the smaller buildings, a lot more of them are owner-occupied. It wouldn't hurt to test and see where you're more effective. If you present yourself better in person than on the phone, evaluate all of your activities and see. But I would do both if it's something you're just starting to do, then evaluate it and improve on your skills, both in person and over the phone. Definitely do both for awhile. I always go to the phone first because I can get more people in an hour than I can by driving around town to see people.

Jim: One thing that I liked about walking in on people is I felt there was a higher probability that I would get in to talk to the decision maker if I was in their office physically, because I just think it's easier to dismiss somebody and put me into voicemail when I'm calling you on the phone, versus when you're standing in reception and waiting to meet with the decision maker.

But today, walking in on people like that can be more difficult the larger the company is that you're calling on. If you're calling on a major industrial building, and there are multiple vice presidents of different departments in there, they may require you to set an appointment in advance.

However, when you're talking about entrepreneurial business owners, I've always felt there was a higher probability that you can get to talk to them in person, as compared to if you called them on the telephone. But at the same time you can probably make a lot more phone calls per hour than the number of people you can meet face-to-face by walking in on them, so it just depends on putting all those things together that we just talked about, and deciding what's best for you.

Mike: We've both made money both ways, right Jim?

Jim: Yes, and it's funny. Something just came into my mind about a guy that I used to coach who's been in the business now for decades. He told me that when he first began his training with a well-known entrepreneurial brokerage company in Los Angeles, that the guy who owned the company told him to go out and knock on doors, and to not come back until he was thrown out at least twice from people's offices. [laughing] I think the idea was to get the new agent to push the envelope so that he'd learn exactly where that fine line was.

Thanks for the question, Len.

The next question comes from Sean. Sean, please go ahead.

Sean: Thank you. How can I differentiate myself so that people will want to work with me over my competitors?

Jim: That's a very good question. Let's do it the same way, Mike. I'll give my answer and then I'll ask you for your comments, too.

There are so many different things involved in answering that, and part of this speaks to what we were talking about earlier today around presentation skills. I mean, do you present yourself as someone they would want to work with ahead of your competitors? I've mentioned from time-to-time that occasionally over the years I've had residential agents come and knock on my door to talk to me when I'm at home, and when I open the door I begin evaluating them. I begin asking myself the question, "Would I want to work with this person, or not?"

I remember one time there was a woman who came to the door, and she was walking her dog at the same time, and it just felt a little too casual for me. Between both that and her presentation style I began thinking to myself, "You know, if I was looking to buy or sell a home right now, I wouldn't tell this person, because I'd really want to work with someone else. I don't want to tell this agent that I'm looking to do anything, because then I've got to remove their teeth marks from my arm with them gripping onto me and telling me, 'No, no, please work with me. I promise I'll do a good job for you.'"

In commercial real estate, when you have people canvassing in the same territory, whether it's on the phone or in person, you could have two brokers canvassing the exact same people over a week or over a month, and come back with different results on the number of leads they've produced. This is because if people don't like your presentation skills, they'll just tell you they're not looking to do anything, even though they may be looking to do something. Whereas the other broker who presents himself or herself more professionally will get the person to open up and then tell them that there's a lead.

It took me awhile to realize this, and then I had a direct experience of it myself with somebody knocking on my door. So presentation skills come into play in terms of both differentiating yourself, but also in terms of what you're doing with your marketing. Are you sending mailing pieces out to people with good, helpful information about what's going on in the market, along with your photo on it, so that they remember you and feel that they already know you? This is definitely much more powerful than only making phone calls, when they never see you.

When you send out good information and mailers that are educating your people, you begin feeling like a consultant or an advisor to them. Then they can start thinking over time, "You know, this is the broker I should probably work with when we have a requirement," and that's what you want to begin accomplishing. You want to position yourself in their mind so that when you call them they're saying something similar to, "Oh, it's you! I've been getting your mailers, and it's nice to talk to you. Yes, we're looking to do something, and your call is very timely."

This is a very different experience when compared to calling them and they have no idea who you are, or they don't remember who you are if you've already spoken with them. In this situation they're asking themselves the question, "Who is this person and why should I be doing business with them?"

That's not a very powerful place to begin initiating your phone conversation with them from.

Mike, do you have anything that you'd like to add?

Mike: Yes, I think that #1 you have to look professional. That's the first thing. You have to look professional, you have to act professional, and then you have to be able to speak like a professional. Then you need to have versatility, like we talked about earlier with Neurolinguistic Programming, so you can have them feel comfortable, and it takes the edge off. I think all of that is a solid package, and we continually have to work on ourselves as a package.

Jim: Absolutely. And Neurolinguistic Programming, for people who may not be familiar with it, is also known as NLP. I know Mike's a big fan and a student of it. I'm a Master Practitioner and a Certified Trainer of it, and it's just amazing what you can do when you learn this approach at a very deep level, in terms of building rapport with people and then moving them towards wanting to do business with you. It's just phenomenal!

That book that I mentioned earlier, *Unlimited Selling Power: How to Master Hypnotic Selling Skills* by Donald Moine and Kenneth Lloyd, is exactly within that arena. It's about talking to the person's unconscious mind so that they just naturally feel like they want to move forward and do business with you. If you haven't read that book, I highly recommend it.

So Sean, did everything we just said answer your question?

Sean: Yes, you've given me some very important things to think about. Thank you.

Jim: OK. So now it's time for us to wrap-up the teleconference. Mike, I want to say thanks so much for joining us and being on the call tonight. Do you have anything you want to say in wrapping-up?

Mike: I could say a lot, but how much time have we got? [laughing] I have some points I just want to kind of recap on here. It's a numbers game, so we must talk to a lot of people every day, and we should know our numbers and know the source of our business, and evaluate that on a regular basis, and then work the numbers to our advantage.

Don't take the rejection personally. It's not about you. There's so much going on in people's lives that you don't know about, and it's not about you.

I would highly recommend that you record your calls so at least you get a chance to hear what you're doing, what you're saying, and how people are responding to you.

Literally, when you find the right people, they really want you to lead them, so as a salesperson it's about asking the right questions. There are powerful questions we can ask them over the phone in order to better lead them.

Then, have a purpose or a "what for" in your life, something that gets you up in the morning that really gets you excited. I get excited when I'm listening to my goals. I'm at the gym, I'm working out, I'm hearing all of this great stuff that I'm doing this year, and it just motivates me.

So have a purpose!

Design a plan of action. Work that plan every day, and part of that plan definitely involves prospecting.

Get a coach. Get some coaching, get some support, and get in accountability mode. Accountability will make things happen immediately!

Again, I'll remind you that there are three ways to generate business: You either wait for it, you buy it, or you go after it. I choose to go after it, and that's my prospecting mode that I get into every day.

Make sure you're putting 80% of your time into the most effective areas... prospecting, lead follow-up, setting appointments, and negotiating contracts, and then put the last 20% into doing administrative work.

Always ask yourself the following question during the day, "What's the best use of my time right now?" That always gets me refocused.

Start each day at zero. Fill that pipeline. If you have four deals in escrow, where's the next one going to come from? It's going to come because you're consistently prospecting every day.

I always remember the STP: See The People.

And the ABCs: Always Be Closing.

And I'll leave you with that.

Jim: That was great! I think that's the most focused and detailed statement that anyone's ever made when I've asked them if there's anything they'd like to say in wrapping up. That was wonderful! Those are great ideas for people to really live by in their brokerage businesses.

Well, that's it. Thanks to everyone for being on the call tonight, and I look forward to speaking with you again the next time.

INTERVIEW 2

Building Solid Relationships With Your Commercial Real Estate Clients

Jim: Tonight, I will be interviewing our special guest, William Hugron, SIOR and CCIM, and with that being said, let me get into my introduction for William.

William Hugron, SIOR and CCIM, has been a commercial real estate agent since 1976, and he's worked in different facets of the commercial real estate industry. Before becoming a commercial broker, he was in property management and in asset management, which gives him a great perspective on what owners and property managers really want to see in a broker in order to list with them.

He has been Vice President of Citicorp and Cal Fed in addition to being Vice President of the Peregrine Real Estate Trust and the Cal REIT Real Estate Investment Trust. William focuses on office, industrial, retail, and land transactions in both California and in the Southwest United States in his brokerage business, and he typically closes more than 75 transactions a year.

With that being said, please join me in welcoming onto our call tonight William Hugron. Willy, thanks for being with us here.

Willy: Thank you for having me.

Jim: Just for everybody here, William goes by the nickname Willy, so I will be calling him by that name tonight because we've known each other for a long time.

In getting into this, one of the main subjects we want to focus on here is relationships. So what do you think is really important for commercial brokers to recognize when it comes to building solid relationships with their clients and prospects?

Willy: Well, everybody talks about social media and the internet, but this is a people relationship business. People do business with people they like, know, understand, and trust. They like working with people who have similar interests.

Jim: I was thinking about this earlier today because I'm actually writing a webinar to do for one of the well-known national companies, so we talk about prospecting and we talk about building relationships, and then there's that aspect of going from identifying the prospect all the way up through getting them committed to working with you exclusively, and then closing the transaction with them. That's a whole different thing than just identifying the prospect alone. This is something that we definitely want to get into tonight because you not only want to find the leads, but you want to build the relationship with people so that they're sold on working with you above and beyond any other broker who they could be working with.

I find that there is a big pitfall and a gap sometimes with the veteran brokers who have closed so many transactions throughout their careers, but they haven't been building the relationships after they've closed the transactions, and they've dropped out all communication. Other brokers are getting in better relationship with their people than they are, and the other brokers are oftentimes in a better position to close their next transaction with them.

With that being said, how much repeat business do you think brokers could actually obtain from people if they became outstanding at building solid, long-term relationships with them?

Willy: Well, they can do a lot of business, but you have to realize that one of two things happens to most businesses. I don't care if it's office, industrial, retail, land, or a lease or sale. If it does well, they will grow and expand. If they don't do well, they're going to need to right-size. In either case, they're going to need you.

Very few professions can stay stagnant. A dentist is an exception, and even then they have a tendency to get more dentists in there.

A retailer or a manufacturer is going to have movement. In life there is always change, and how you deal with it is going to make it or break it.

Jim: I was actually making a presentation at an office last week, and one of the things that came up when I was talking to them was that you have to stay in contact with the people that you've closed your past transactions with, because you might have sold a building to somebody or made a five-year lease with a company and you're thinking, "Wait a second. They're not going to need anything for five years, so I really don't need to talk to them for a while."

But sometimes, two or three years into it they can all of a sudden decide that they need more space. You're thinking, "I've got two more years before I need to talk to them," and then they work with the first broker who grabs their attention. So you really need to be in regular contact with these people after you close transactions with them, don't you?

Willy: Absolutely.

Jim: Why do you think it is that so many brokers close transactions with their people and then they completely drop out all communication with them?

Willy: They're so focused on closing the deals they have in their hand that they don't put time into marketing or improving their pipeline. It's a really common phenomenon. You're so intense on what you're doing. It's self-management and time-management. You have to put some time aside every week to focus on marketing and getting new people because when you close your deals, what do you have left? You always have to keep the pipeline full.

Jim: I heard one broker say, "I finally realized years ago that every time I close my next transaction, I'm basically unemployed."

Ideally, you want to have a number of things in the pipeline, but I get it. It's like, "They're done for right now." They're not going to need anything for a certain period of time, and you have to follow up with what is on your plate right now and follow up on bringing in some more business.

What can brokers expect to happen when they drop out all communication with their past clients like this?

Willy: The old saying holds true, "Out of sight, out of mind." If you're not in contact or in communication with someone, they're going to forget about you.

Jim: Yes.

Willy: There are ways you can stay in contact with your clients by offering services. I have a law firm client who I've had for years. I'm going to talk about this client many times because several things are going to be very appropriate. They won't sign a document without me reviewing it.

They have several leases throughout the state of California. Every time they get an estoppel or a rent increase or an operating pass, they always pass it through me. I don't get paid to do that, but I get so much business from them that it pays for the results. It's about service, but it also exemplifies what you just illustrated: I stay in contact with them. They know me. They rely on me. They trust me, and they're the attorneys.

I say, "You guys are the attorneys. Why are you asking me all the time?" But I say that to myself, and to them I say, "I'm glad to be of service."

It's my way of being in contact and helping them all the time. I'm their go-to person.

Jim: I think that's great because usually we think in terms of clients wanting to run something by their attorney first instead of signing it, and you've got a law firm and they say that they want to run it by you. That's great!

Willy: Relationships are built on trust and rapport. I try to build a relationship with rapport, and that's a good example.

They get bombarded by brokers cold-calling them all the time, and they refer them all to me.

Jim: That's great! That's where you want to be. I talk with people about how ideally you want to work on your business such that with the people you've closed transactions with, you build the kind of relationship where you become their broker for life, where they're sold on you and they want to always run things by you like what you're talking about. That takes special relationship-building skills, because unlike somebody's CPA or attorney who they deal with throughout the year on different financial and legal matters, brokers need to create the feeling that there is still a relationship in place, even though they may have recently closed a transaction and the client may be years away from closing their next transaction. That takes the kind of business-building relationship skills that we're talking about right here.

So instead of dropping out all communication with their people after they've closed a transaction with them, give us some ideas on what brokers should be doing instead to help to build and solidify the relationship.

Willy: One thing that I do with all my clients every year is I give them an annual Christmas card. I sold a law firm a small office condo in Anaheim, and I just kept in touch with them by sending them a Christmas card along with my business card. A couple of the attorneys retired and they wanted to sell. They called me up and said, "The only reason why we're calling you is because you stayed in touch with us with your Christmas cards."

It's inexpensive, it's a routine, and I'm really particular in how I do this. All my Christmas cards go out the day after Thanksgiving, and I'm always the first card that they get. Life is about experiences and memories, and I want to be the first one, and I always do it.

I send them out and I always write a little note in there so I'm not just signing the card. I try to personalize it. The Christmas card thing has really paid off for me.

What happens is these people are retiring, they want to sell, and they call me up.

Jim: I think that's phenomenal that you're getting such great results from Christmas cards alone, but I'm thinking that two to four times a year it would be relatively easy with today's technology for a broker to send out cards to the people they've closed transactions with, thanking them for their business, asking them if there's anything they can do for them right now, and to please give them a call if there is. Just say that it's wonderful being your commercial real estate broker, implying that there is still a relationship in place. I think doing something like that two to four times a year would be wonderful on top of calling them just to check in to see how they're doing, and this will help to build and keep that relationship in place.

I think that's great what you're doing with the Christmas cards. By the way, Willy, something that I actually chatted with you about a little bit before the call, I think this is the perfect opportunity--because I want to make sure that we get this story in here--is to talk about your Rolls Royce story.

You have a classic car collection, and I know for people who have been with me for years as a member and as a coaching client, they've heard about this. But for people who haven't, I just think it will be great for them to hear this story.

Tell us about what you do with that special Rolls Royce and the people that you want to solidify your relationship with at the next level.

Willy: I try to incorporate my social activities with my business. We'll go into more detail on that, but I try to build relationships with clients, and I try to create experiences.

I join clubs. I belong to a half-dozen car clubs. I get involved in these clubs and I get to know people. I have volunteered in positions, and then people get to know me. I don't tell them what I do right away. I don't want to be like that network marketer guy who tries to get everybody to sign up for their program.

I build the relationship, build the rapport, let them know what I do, and try to be of service for them. Then I try to create memories.

Before I get into the Rolls Royce story, I want to do something else. One thing that I do is when I close a deal, whether it's a lease or a sale, I have the tenant and the landlord or the buyer and the seller meet me at the property. I tell them that I'm going to do a toast.

What I do is I set up a little table and I have a tray with some champagne glasses. I have a saber sword and a bottle of champagne, and I open the bottle of champagne with the saber sword. I tell them the history of it.

Well, it only takes 10 minutes to do, and it doesn't cost me much, and it's a memory that no other broker does. You want to set yourself apart from all the other brokers. They're really excited about this, and they remember me.

The other thing I do, as Jim mentioned, is I have an antique Rolls Royce, and I belong to the Rolls Royce club, and I've served on the board. I was both Vice Chair and Chair.

If you have an antique car, your antique car insurance is really cheap. In addition, there's an organization out here where you can hire a driver to drive your car.

So when I close a big deal, in addition to the saber sword I tell the clients that I'm going to have a car come to their house, take them and their spouse out to dinner, and then drive them home or wherever they want to go. Well, they automatically think it's going to be a limo, and what shows up is a white classic Rolls Royce. They remember that.

They go out to dinner and I pick up the tab. It doesn't cost me much. It's about $150 for the driver and a few hundred for dinner, but it's a memory that they will always remember, and it sets me apart from the pack.

Jim: What year is the Rolls Royce?

Willy: It's a 1958 Silver Cloud One.

Jim: That's the type of thing they'll remember, especially the people that you're sending this car for who are at least in their mid-40's if not 50's or 60's, right?

Willy: Correct.

Jim: So now here's the idea of something classic like that. Who gets a limo experience with a beautiful classic Rolls Royce these days? It's always whatever the limo of the day is right now that people get the experience of, especially for people in their 40's and beyond. It's that sense of class and vintage that's been around and consistent, along with the classic Rolls Royce name. Driving down the street, people are going to be turning heads looking at the car as opposed to where we live here in Southern California, and their reactions to normal limousines are like, "Yeah, so what?"

But that car is going to turn heads and leave an amazing impression on the people who you do this for. I just think it's wonderful and so unique, and I applaud you for it.

Willy: I also want to share another story similar to this one. A friend of mine from the Rolls Royce club had a couple of assisted living facilities in Santa Monica that he had listed with another broker. The other broker's listing expired, and they didn't sell it.

I asked my friend, "Hey, can you give me a shot at it?"

He said, "I'll give you a pocket listing."

I said, "Fine." So I immediately joined forces with somebody I knew who specialized in assisted living. We immediately put it in escrow, sold both of them for $18 million, and the client was really happy. But there are a couple of lessons here. We'll get into more detail later, but if you don't specialize in a particular product type, don't do it yourself; join forces with someone and get help. Getting part of something is better than getting all of nothing.

Then the story continues, and it got even better. The seller's attorney called me up a year later and said, "How would you like to have a $30 million listing on some other assisted living facilities?"

I said, "Sure." So I immediately contacted the guy who I hooked-up with before to list three different facilities, two of which were in Santa Barbara, and it ended up being a $50 million listing--all because of a relationship with someone that I met in the car club. I didn't go out trying to get business; I built a relationship first. But now it's turning into phenomenal business.

Jim: That's wonderful because when you can spend your time socializing among the type of people who are going to be the decision makers that you want to do business with, that's phenomenal. When you come in from a social aspect, be it a club like that or a charity, you don't have the same resistance in the person as if you're trying to make a cold-call to them. If you get involved in committees or things like that, you can now have the OK to call them on behalf of business for the organization, which is another great way to come in through the back door or side door to start building that relationship.

With what you just said, this is a perfect example of it. You don't want to get in there and start running around handing your business cards out to people--as you said--and announcing yourself. It's all about the care of the organization and what is best for the organization, coordinating with people, being on committees, and through that type of relationship building in a social environment, it can lead to tremendous business like the kind of transactions you were just mentioning.

Willy: I want to mention a couple of other things on that subject. We all go to these functions, and I've noticed that certain people know how to work the crowd. Most people are nervous and shy and uncomfortable. The people who go up and introduce themselves and say, "Hi, my name is Willy," and start building a conversation, you're breaking the ice and breaking the barriers. I don't go in there and start telling them what I do, so you're just building rapport and talking to them.

It takes a lot of courage just to take the initiative and go up to people and approach them, but you would be surprised at the reaction. People are very relieved and pleased that you're talking to them. It's a scary thing to do, but you've got to get out of your comfort level. You'll make more relationships and contacts that way.

Jim: Something I wanted to mention also, going back to what you talked about earlier with the saber sword and the champagne, I believe you have a video on YouTube about that, too, don't you? Assuming it's still there, what key words should people search under to find the video where you're opening the champagne bottle with the saber sword?

Willy: "William Hugron saber master". If you just look under "William Hugron" you'll see a bunch of stuff on me, and my YouTube video will show up. I encourage you to go look at it. It's professionally done in a studio, and it tells the whole history behind it. It doesn't take long, and it's entertaining.

Jim: I've seen the video, and it's a very unique idea. I have to believe that sometimes when you're doing it in front of the building along with the two principals that you must be turning some heads of the people just walking by, or driving by.

Willy: Absolutely. First thing, people are a little intimidated with the sword. The sword isn't that long. It's a special sword for this purpose.

Jim: It's just so unique. Between that and the Rolls Royce story, those are two amazing out of the box ideas!

I know that in some major cities, for people listening thinking, "That's great, but I don't have a classic car collection or a Rolls Royce," there are some places where you can rent or get limo rides in classic cars, so that is an alternative for you also if you are interested in doing this and matching it up with the kind of people you'd like to give this kind of experience to.

So this is all about building relationships and getting repeat business from people. So when you get repeat business, Willy, and you close transactions with people the second, third, and fourth time, what does that feel like as compared to having to hustle with people for the first time to close business with them? It's a nicer situation for you, isn't it?

Willy: Well, hopefully these people are people you've made relationships with, you've built rapport with them, and you have a connection with them. It's more like being a friend. It's just so much easier.

All the barriers are broken down, and you have a rapport and a trust that makes it much easier to do business. Yes, it's very enjoyable.

One other thing that I want to mention is when you meet people and you talk to people, one thing that I've learned is to be excited and passionate about what you're doing and what you're talking about. Being passionate becomes contagious. People want to do business with people who are upbeat and positive. I like what I do, and I make no bones about it. I mean, I enjoy what I do and I want to help people. I have fun doing it, and people want to be around that environment and that type of person.

Jim: There was a guy who passed away last year who I loved listening to, and watching his videos and reading his books--a guy named Wayne Dyer. He used to say that when you're in sales and you're really passionate, excited, and enthusiastic about what you're doing, people aren't really buying into the product or service you're selling, they're buying into your excitement and your level of enthusiasm.

Willy: It goes back to being in a people/relationship business.

Jim: However you are behaving and talking to people, you are impacting their mental and emotional state. You want to make it a positive impact and ideally get them excited and happy to be around you instead of just communicating, "You wouldn't want to sell your building, would you?"

You are in the position where you are going to be changing and impacting their state, and when they feel that positivity, they want to be around you more.

Make sure that you're in that kind of state when you're talking to your people--especially when you're prospecting because they don't know you from anybody in the beginning--but ideally be this way with everybody including your clients and prospects, too.

We talked about repeat business. What percentage of your own business today would you estimate comes from actually working with people you've already closed transactions with?

Willy: About 90% of my business is repeat and referral business. By that I mean that not only are they people I've done business with, but people I'm involved with.

I'm involved with all these organizations. So is that repeat business? Well, yes and no. I have interactions in different ways, and so it's kind of like repeat business in a way. Maybe I'm doing business from one level and doing business on a different level, but it's repeat business. It's a relationship.

Jim: How many different organizations are you a member of?

Willy: I belong to six car clubs, and I have 15 real estate designations. I started my career with property management designations, and then I went to broker designations, and then besides the CCIM and SIOR designations I have four of the six designations that ICSC offers. Then when I belong to these organizations, I have your typical type-A personality.

When I got my CCIM designation, I got on the board. Then I became Chapter President. With the Rolls Royce club it was the same thing. First I got on the board, and then I was the Vice-Chair and then Chair.

You just get into the top, and that's how you get involved and meet people. Then all of a sudden relationships occur, and you have trust and they will do business with you.

In terms of real estate, I belong to about 15 organizations. With cars, I belong to six. It keeps me busy.

Jim: Wow! When you're becoming a member of these organizations or beginning to show up at their meetings, this is something that people will recognize as being your typical Chamber of Commerce situation. People will oftentimes go to these meetings thinking, "Well, I just want to be able to show up and go to these meetings, and hopefully tons of business will just come my way," and it's not going to happen that way. There are so many people at those kinds of meetings with the same attitude of, "I just want the business to come to me."

No, you've got to ideally get involved in the organization and show that you care about the organization, and meet people in a social context and show them that you care. Maybe even get involved as a Chair of something or on a committee or something like that. With your regular Chamber of Commerce, you've got to get involved. Otherwise people aren't just going to come to you and say, "Oh, you sell real estate. Great! We want to start working with you."

It just doesn't work that way. So I think it's great that you're talking about this and how important it is to pursue the social aspect of it, and not just lead with, "Hey, I'm a real estate agent. Do you have any business for me?"

Willy: Like I said earlier, when you go to these things, go up to people and introduce yourself, and just build rapport. People don't always do that. But the people who do really get the benefit out of it.

For every action, there is a reaction. What you put out there is what you'll get back. Communication is the same way. Be careful what you say because how they respond may not be the way that you want.

Talk to them in a nice, friendly manner. Be approachable, and break some ice barriers.

Jim: Interestingly, Willy, I just recently read for the first time Dale Carnegie's *How to Win Friends and Influence People*. I'm guessing you've read the book. I didn't read it because I remember the ads from decades ago that were in black and white and they showed businessmen dressed like they were from the 1950s or 1960s, and in my mind I kept thinking, "This book has got to be so out of date. Why would I read it?"

Enough people that I respected told me that they had read it, and then I read it within the last 30 days, and it's very, very good. I was surprised that I read things in there that I hadn't really heard anybody say in all those years since that book was first written, and it was written back in the 1930s. I hadn't really read a number of things that they talked about in other forms in other books. It may exist, but I just haven't read the books....and I read a lot of books!

They talk about taking an interest in somebody. Instead of just telling them who you are, find out about them. Everybody would much rather have somebody take an interest in them and be curious about them, rather than you trying to tell them who you are and what's important to you.

Sometimes people say that a person talks too much, but I jokingly say if you could ever have somebody say, "You listen too much," that would be a tremendous compliment. I recommend that people read the book if they've never read it before.

Willy: People like to talk about themselves, and sometimes you have to ask questions in order for people to answer. You ask questions that don't have 'yes/no' answers. Once people start going, and once you break the ice and start asking questions and they start talking, what I'm learning in life is that less is more. The less I say, the better off I am. The more I listen, I become a better listener and learn how to ask even better questions.

Once people can open up, they will relate to you automatically. They will think you're on the same level. It's just phenomenal once you start learning to work the crowd, going up to people, talking to them, asking them questions, and listening to them. You'll break the barriers and break the ice.

Jim: One of the things that the book said, among the many other great things that were in there, was it talked about really trying to do everything you can to make sure that you don't get in an argument with somebody. Even in the end, you may walk away feeling that you proved your point, and that they were wrong and you were right, but almost all the time the other person is going to still feel that they were right and you were wrong. So you just end up angry at the other side, and having them want to do business with you less, or like you even less as a person.

The book talks about different ways to basically move down that path to resolution instead of possibly locking antlers over a particular subject. You definitely would rather be doing business than getting in an argument with somebody.

Actually, let me mention one other thing, too. I found a version of the book on Amazon--the Kindle version--by one of the publishers for only $2.99. So if you're interested in the book and you like reading digitally, the Kindle version may still hopefully be available for $2.99 if that's any incentive for you to go and buy the book.

We've talked about repeat business, but let's talk about identifying a prospect and then moving down the path of solidifying that person wanting to do business with you and close a transaction.

So from the moment you first identify the prospect, talk to us about some of the steps along the way that you feel are important to get them closer and closer to wanting to work with you exclusively on their next transaction.

Willy: In order to receive, you've got to give first, and you always have to give with an offer. Most owners, and it doesn't matter if it's cars or real estate, always feel like their asset is worth more than it is, and they always want to know what the market is and what is going on.

I always find out what they own, and then I try to give them market information on their property, even if they have it listed with another broker. I'm not trying to get the listing now. I just offer them information. You want to be the go-to person in any market. You want to be able to know what's on the market and what's selling. When something sells, I let that person know, "This sold for this price." If a new property comes on the market for sale or for lease, I let them know, "Hey, this came on the market," or I give them several properties.

People like that information. You're offering information, not advice. You're not telling them and you're not trying to sell them anything; you're just giving information. You're showing them that you're an expert in your market, in your niche, in your field. That usually goes a long way.

Jim: Absolutely.

Willy: They will call you and ask you questions.

Jim: It kind of touches on what we talked about earlier in terms of showing an interest in them and doing what shows that you're taking care of them, i.e., showing them information that can tell them what their building is worth right now. Because every owner would like to know what their building is worth right now, especially if you can somehow tell them that it's worth more than they thought. In a rising market, you can do that. In other markets, it's a lot harder to do. Basically you just want to show them that you really care.

Willy: One thing I used to do is when I noticed something that wasn't right on their property, I would take some digital photographs and I would download it on a mini CD. We don't use CDs much anymore, so I would do it on a thumb drive. On the CD I would have a label with their name, their address, my name, my phone number, and I would send it to them and say, "Hey, I noticed this on your property. You might want to take a look at this."

I don't tell them that it's bad or wrong; I just say, "I noticed this, and I don't know if you're aware of this."

That has come back to me in dividends beyond belief. A mini CD is not something they're used to seeing. Now I know most computers can't handle them, but it's the thought that I went out of my way, took a picture, downloaded it onto a CD, and sent it to them with a label with my contact information. I do that also when I close a deal. I download all the information onto a CD with all the documents along with my name and phone number so that they have a whole file just on a CD, and they keep that and remember me.

Jim: That's good. They're not going to want to toss that because they know all the documents are in there and it has your name and contact information on there. Now you're giving them something where they go, "We have to put this in a place where we know where it is for the future, for when we may want to access it again."

That's good.

Willy: We're providing value.

Jim: Absolutely. Again, it's that little extra level of service and care that most brokers won't necessarily do.

Let's talk for a moment about listing presentation packages. I'm curious as to how long your listing presentation packages are and what kind of information you include in there.

Willy: A couple of things. We talked about communication. There's a term called "mirroring". You want to mirror what the other person is saying or doing. Well, it's the same thing when I'm doing a listing presentation. I try to figure out who I'm giving the presentation to. If it's a mom and pop, they're not going to want an encyclopedia; they're going to want the bare-bone facts as much as possible. Some fluff, but not too much.

If you're going to be dealing with an institution, and as Jim mentioned, I used to be an asset manager for Cal Fed and Citicorp--in those major organizations, decisions are never made by one person; it's always by a committee. The committee will make decisions based on the fact that they have done their due diligence, have done their homework, and they've covered themselves so no one can point a finger to them and say, "Why did you do this?"

If I'm going to do a presentation to an institution where the final action is going to be decided by a committee, I'm going to have a big book with lots of documentation, back-up, and support so no one can point a finger and say, "You didn't address that; you didn't do this or that." It's all there and it's all documented.

So mom and pops would be a small listing package, and a big institution would be a big listing package and a big presentation.

Another really important thing: When I was an asset manager, I used to give RFPs to brokers, and I would want them to answer my questions. This is embarrassing, but I can't tell you how many times brokers would not answer all my questions in my RFP. These brokers were eliminated automatically, right away.

Before you ask for the listing, ask questions and find out what they want to know and what they want to hear if they don't already have the questions ahead of time.

I ask a lot of questions and then I find out what is important to them, and I give them what they want. It's not what I want; it's about them. How can I be of service to them?

Jim: Absolutely. I'm sure most people know what RFP means, but just in case somebody is scratching their head, it stands for Request for Proposal. Every now and then, Willy, I hear a new acronym I haven't heard before and I have to ask what it is because the industry keeps inventing more of them.

So how soon after a broker has closed a transaction with a client do you think they should begin contacting them again?

Willy: During the transaction. They should always ask for a referral during the transaction when they're in the honeymoon period. There's a concept that I want to go into detail on. The concept is called "being in the conversation". Before you bought your last car, you started asking people questions, you started reading about it, and looking into it. As soon as you started getting focused on a certain car, you saw that particular car everywhere.

Well, the same thing happens to someone who is going to lease or buy property. They start talking to other people and asking them questions, and all of a sudden they're in a circle of people who are in the same place they are. They're in the conversation of buying or selling or leasing, and those people are in contact with people who are in the market.

Sometimes they already have brokers; sometimes they don't. So I'm a firm believer of asking for a referral during the transaction when everybody is happy and in the honeymoon, and everything is going good and strong. There are no problems arising, and they're talking to other people. This is phenomenal timing.

Jim: Absolutely. Here's a way that that can be done, and you just need to feel when it's the right time. It could be as you're moving forward to close the transaction, or it could be at a celebratory lunch or dinner afterward. There's just a moment in time when you feel that it's right and you're in good rapport, and everybody is feeling warm and fuzzy. You can just say something like, "Stan, I've loved working with you, and truth be told, I'd love to work with more people who are just like you. So my question to you is, 'Who do you know who may be looking to buy, sell, or lease commercial real estate?'"

Let me just mention the components of what I just said. When you say, "Stan, I've loved working with you," you're paying Stan a compliment which ideally puts him in a place of feeling even warmer and fuzzier towards you, and it puts him in a position of ideally wanting to reciprocate the compliment. Then as you say that you would love to work with more people just like him, again it's a compliment in terms of how highly you regard him, his personality, your relationship with him, and your experience in working with him.

Then you say, "Who do you know who may be looking to buy, sell, or lease commercial real estate?" This is a very important way of wording it because it bypasses asking a yes or no question. You're not saying, "Stan, do you know anybody who is looking to buy, sell, or lease?" When you say that, it's easy for Stan to say, "No". We as people are trained innately to say no in situations like that just to get off the hook from trying to think of any names to give the person.

When you say, "Who do you know?" instead, you're basically presupposing that Stan knows somebody. Now you're asking him basically to come up with one or more names, assuming that he already knows somebody. Since you complimented him in the beginning, it helps to stack the deck within his emotions along with the warm feelings to have him go, "Yeah, who do I know? I've just been paid a nice compliment. It would be nice to at least give one name back to this person. Who do I know?"

Let me take it one step further. When you get names from people like that; when you get on the phone and call the referral and say, "I was out to lunch with Stan. We just sold his building, and he told me to call you because he's been doing business with you for so long. He thought I should check in with you and see if you're looking to do anything."

The person will go, "Oh, you know Stan? Stan and I go back 20 years in doing business together." You come into an amazingly warm situation as compared with if you had cold-called the person. It's totally different now that you're coming in through your relationship with Stan, and they treat you differently because you're coming in through Stan, and you're coming in with the credibility of the relationship that they already have attached to Stan.

So just keep that in mind in terms of the timing, and exactly what you say and how you ask the question.

In addition, something that I've mentioned before is when you close a transaction with somebody, you could say, "Listen, here's something I'd like to do for you. I'd like to get you and all the key employees out in front of the building and we'll take a nice photo. I'll pay for this. I'll put this on a postcard, and we'll send it to everybody that you do business with, basically announcing your new location and your new address and phone number, telling everybody that you've moved."

So now when they give you the database of who to send it to, now you know that these people know Stan. So then I can make note in my own database of the people who know Stan, and then when I'm doing my prospecting I can say to them, "Hey, Bill," or, "Hey, Kathy, we're the people who moved Stan into that building over on Main Street."

"Oh, that's you guys?" they might say. "Oh, we got the postcard. That's wonderful."

Again, now you're coming in through the relationship with Stan because you're bringing up the fact that you helped move his company to their new location. Again, that's huge when you can call tens or hundreds of people knowing that you have that connection with Stan that you can bring into the conversation, telling them that you just sold Stan his building. It's a good approach, and it's also a heartfelt gift of sending out the postcards for the people you just closed the transaction with.

So with you personally, Willy, how much prospecting are you doing yourself these days?

Willy: I'm doing some different things in prospecting. First of all, I've hired an intern who is doing a lot of my social media marketing. I'm starting to do more of that, which I have not done before. The reason I'm doing that is the residential brokers are always ahead of the commercial brokers. On the residential side, I think it's up to 85% of people are going online to look for a residential place before they buy. On the commercial side, the statistics are showing a substantial increase in commercial buyers or tenants going online to look for product.

I'm trying to address that. Like I said earlier, change is inevitable, and how you deal with it. I'm trying to deal with change as much as I can.

I'm also sending out postcards.

Now here's an important issue. It takes eight or nine contacts to create credibility with people. As Jim mentioned, I do office, industrial, retail, and land. I do nothing with beds. If it has a bed, I don't touch it.

Years ago I was doing tons of land transactions, and I want to get back into that because it was fun. So there's a particular farm I've identified, and I'm trying to be the go-to expert. I'm sending out postcards and letters, and I'm sending out information like, "Here's what is going on in the market. Here is something that just came on the market. This just sold."

I'm trying to provide information to people, and what these people do with these postcards, they don't always need me right then and there, but with consistency and repetition they're realizing that I'm consistent and I'm active in the area. They put these postcards in a folder, and then when they need me, they go to that folder. I've seen that happen.

It doesn't get an immediate response, but in the long-term it gets you lots of response. They also consider me as the expert and the go-to person because I'm always providing them information and I'm staying up-to-date, and I'm consistent.

You see this a lot in residential tracts where you own your own home. You might get a new agent in the area who sends you out one or two postcards, and then you don't hear from them anymore. The agent who is consistently sending them out year after year, they're the one who gets all the business.

Jim: Absolutely.

Willy: They're considered the go-to expert. So I'm doing two things: I'm experimenting with social media; I hired a college intern who is doing a lot of this for me. And I'm doing this postcard campaign in a particular area because I've had success in that area before.

Jim: I remember years ago, in the area that I grew up in, Santa Monica, California, my father passed away and I was going over to the house to spend time with my mother quite a bit, making sure that she was OK. I was collecting the mail and everything, and I would see the postcards that the agents were sending.

All of a sudden, this new agent in the area started sending two postcards a month...very well done, professional, and with good copy. I just looked at this, and within a matter of two to four months I just went, "Wow! If I needed to call an agent to sell my mother's house at any moment in time, or if I needed any more information, I would definitely call this person." They made a tremendous impression on me in such a short period of time, as compared with all the other veterans in the territory who weren't doing any mailing, or who were doing very little mailing.

It just goes to show you, especially in commercial, because so few brokers mail at all or they mail once in a blue moon and they just don't want to spend the money. They look around their office and they say, "Well, nobody else is mailing, so why should I do it?"

Bad mistake. You get to brand yourself in people's minds like this residential agent who I mentioned. Willy, you're on top of it. You're talking about this. People will take the postcard or the newsletter and they stick it in the property file, and then when they're ready to do something, they pull out the file and they pull the postcard or the mailer out of it, and there's your phone number.

They say, "Madge and I are getting ready to sell, and we really liked this postcard that you sent us eight months ago, and it's in our file. We've got to talk to somebody, and your name jumped out at us from the postcard."

It's just huge. If you're not mailing, it's a big mistake in terms of differentiating yourself from your competitors and getting more business.

Willy: It's important when you do these postcards that you're providing information and value.

Jim: Yes.

Willy: Talk to them about the market. There are vacancy factors. Rates are going up. Concessions are going down if you're leasing. This is what your competition is doing. There are all kinds of things you can say. Just think about not selling, but offering information. Not advice, but information.

Jim: Yes, I tell brokers that you want to become that voice in their head like you're the top expert consultant or advisor in your territory.

I remember hearing a guy saying once in front of an audience that every adult is basically like a child walking around with their umbilical cord in their hand, looking for some expert to plug it into to take them and guide them in the right direction.

In commercial real estate, your owners--just like anybody else in business including people with assets--they're always worrying about things, and if they're making the right decision and what's going on within the market, and is my timing OK and what do I have to be worried about.

When you can take that guiding hand and say, "Look, here's where we're at right now, and here's where we're headed," they're going to love that, because everybody wants to find the magic crystal ball in commercial real estate. If you can take that voice for where the trends are going and what that now means for their future, they're going to love it. You can do that as we've just said through mailing by taking that voice and basically, meta-phorically speaking, being the Paul Revere and riding into town saying, "The British are coming! The British are coming!" Which can translate to, "This is where the market is headed, and I'm the broker who's the expert who can tell you where it's headed."

They want that. They'll love that. They'll line up to do business with you if you provide them with that information and mail it to them regularly.

So tell us who is working along with you in your business and what their job responsibilities are.

Willy: I have a whole team of people. I mentioned I have a college intern, and I really want to take a couple of minutes to talk about college interns.

I have another associate friend of mine from another firm who hires col-lege interns all the time, but he doesn't pay them. I don't believe in that. I believe you pay for what you get. He's had some pretty good results, but they also don't last.

In my opinion, it takes time to teach and train someone. I like to hire college interns, and I like to pay them. What they can do on a computer is a lot faster than what I can do, and it's really worth it.

I also have a lady who is an escrow coordinator who works for me. She handles all my paperwork and escrows to make sure everything is covered and documented. I also have another associate broker agent with me who helps me with leases, who also shows space and does deals.

In addition, we have two support staff in our firm who type up our leases and type up our offers. So we have a whole slew of people who help us. I also have a bookkeeper who works part-time for me who pays all my bills and keeps everything on track in QuickBooks, so when I do my tax returns, it's easy to just give it to my CPA to do my taxes. I consider her part of my team because she keeps everything up-to-date.

There's an expression, "If you don't have an assistant, you are the assistant." Well, that also applies to a bookkeeper. If you don't have a bookkeeper, you are the bookkeeper. That's not the best use of my time. Plus, you want to delegate what you're not good at and focus on what you're good at. Everybody is good at something, and a good manager has to figure out what people are good at and put them in that task. I've learned this over the years, and it's really paid off.

Jim: There are times on different teleconference calls that I do over the years, Willy, where I repeat that quote, "If you don't have an assistant, you are the assistant," and I attribute it to you. It's just one of those quotes that I've heard that I think is so poignant and important.

Let me talk about this for a second. For most people on the call, your time when you're selling and in front of people, and making presentations, and doing your prospecting, and trying to find business, it's worth a significant amount of money. For most people on the call, it's going to be hundreds of dollars an hour at least. But some of you may be going, "Wait a second, that sounds like a lot of money."

Well, it sounds like a lot of money because of all of the other administrative things that you're doing that are not worth hundreds of dollars an hour, and they're taking up so much of your time. So if you can pay somebody to do things for you, and you can pay them $15.00-$40.00 an hour to do many things that you're spending time on right now, you can now take that time and it's now worth hundreds of dollars an hour to you when you're prospecting people and meeting with people and making listing presentations. That's a tremendous trade-off of money for more time, so you can now make much more money with that time you've recaptured.

As Willy said, if you don't have an assistant, then you are the assistant. It means that you're now paying yourself the $15.00-$40.00 an hour because you're doing the assistant's work, and you're missing out on the opportunity to free up that time to generate hundreds of dollars an hour of income with it instead.

You have to understand that trade-off, and it's very dangerous to just look around the office and say, "Well, everybody else is doing the same thing." Just because they're doing that and blindly costing themselves a lot of money, doesn't mean that you should be doing the same thing.

Willy understands this. He gets this. He's got people around him that he's paying, and they're doing great things for him. It's freeing up his time to do the much more valuable stuff on a per hour basis that helps him to make much greater amounts of money.

Willy: I'd like to make two points. As a broker, all I have is my time and my knowledge. How I use my time and my knowledge is going to determine how much money I make.

You have to think smart and wisely. All you have is your time and your knowledge, and how you spend it is going to determine what you make.

Jim: Yes.

Willy: Another point I want to make in terms of delegating, is a lot of people use virtual assistants. A virtual assistant is someone who is not in your office. They work on their own pace on their own time. Virtual assistants are good. I've had people tell me they've had good stories...both good success, and bad success.

I want to make one caveat: If you're going to hire a virtual assistant, make sure they're on the continent. I had a horrible experience with a virtual assistant and with programmers in India and in Russia. Have them be in the United States. People who have used domestic (meaning in the United States) virtual assistants have had much better luck than with people in Russia or in India.

I'm not saying there aren't some good ones there, but I'm saying overall with the time difference and everything else, it doesn't work.

Jim: Let me add something to that also because I became intrigued and started using virtual assistants back in 2002. A friend of mine was basically the guy who brought virtual assistants to the residential real estate industry back then, a guy named Michael Russer. He's a very well-known person on the residential side of the business as a trainer.

I started hiring virtual assistants, and I basically have some caveats, so to speak, that will help you when you're hiring them. Number one, be very wary of virtual assistants who are charging small amounts per hour. What that oftentimes means is they're in-between jobs and they're looking to get hired by a major corporation, and they just want to generate some money while they're interviewing to get the next job.

You ideally want to hire somebody who has already been a virtual assistant for years, showing you that they've made a commitment to being in the industry, rather than being somebody who has only been doing it for several months. Again, they may be looking for another job, and the last thing you want is to hire one or more virtual assistants, and then, weeks or months later, they're gone from the business, and you have to find, hire, and retrain somebody new.

Ideally, if you can find somebody who basically has their own virtual assistant business and they've been doing this for five or ten years or more, that's a great statement they're making that they're going to be around for a longer period of time.

If you are wanting to hire a virtual assistant who is going to be around for the long run, those are some tips that I recommend you follow. If it's somebody who you just want to do one project, then it's a little bit easier to hire somebody who maybe hasn't been around as long, because once the project is done you won't necessarily need them again.

You can hire these people to do marketing for you, postcards, copywriting, design, putting together presentation packages, running comps reports, administrative activities, putting together a database for you, or getting your database to the next level, in addition to doing things like bookkeeping and accounting. There are so many different things that can be done that are support services for real estate agents, and these virtual assistants are available.

Their rates tend to be anywhere between $15.00-$60.00 an hour, depending on who you're talking to and what you want done. Let me just mention a website for this, too: www.IVAA.org. That's the International Virtual Assistants Association. There are people there who have real estate specialty designations who you may want to talk to, which means that they are very likely doing support services for residential agents--and not necessarily commercial--but you'd much rather have somebody who is familiar with working with agents, as opposed to somebody who is not.

In addition, the people located at www.REBackOffice.com specialize in providing virtual assistant services for the commercial real estate industry. So if you think you may want to hire a virtual assistant to help you within your commercial real estate brokerage business, I recommend that you contact them.

Let me mention another resource, too. I believe most people on the call know who Mike Lipsey is. He's a great trainer in our industry, and in terms of traveling and speaking in front of audiences, Mike has done that more than anyone.

When I was an agent myself, I would attend Mike Lipsey trainings. With this in mind, his son has developed his own virtual assistant business for the commercial real estate industry. His son is Jordan, and his website is www.MLJordan.com. You can go to that website, and he's familiar with doing many of the kinds of support services that commercial real estate brokers want to have done. Just chat with him and see if it may be a fit for you when you need these kinds of services.

Willy: I'd like to add one more thing, Jim, if I may. I'd like to talk about runners and broker trainees. I personally have not had success with training brokers. I get asked all the time by them to come work for me, for me to train them, for me to teach them. Here are some of my bad experiences. I've had a couple who I've trained and I've put them on some listings. I had two retail listings in Orange County that I had trained this lady on. They were big centers doing lots of leases, and I trained this lady to do everything.

For a while I wasn't talking to the owners all the time; I was letting her do it. But I was involved in every single transaction and I negotiated every deal and did all the paperwork, or supervised all the paperwork.

After a while the owners said, "We never hear about Willy anymore. Let's take his name off the sign and make sure he doesn't get any of these commissions."

I lost three or four listings from this one client because I had taught and trained this lady so well. She took over my listings, and then when I had that experience I thought, "I'm not doing that again."

We're a small firm, and we don't have a training program for brokers. Large firms like CBRE and Newmark Knight Frank have training programs and they're equipped to handle that.

That may work for them, but I have not had good luck, and I've had a couple of other partners in my firm train people without success, too. But in the defense of the trainee, we don't have a good training program.

In the old days they would say, "Here's a phone book, now cold-call everybody," but I don't believe in that. That is one way of doing business, but it's not the way I want to do business. That's how some people were trained, and some people make it, and some people don't.

I just wanted to make a comment, as we were talking about support staff, and getting people to help on your team. Some people have had luck with training new agents, but in my opinion, most people don't.

Jim: Yes. I've got to tell you, just the number of people who I talk to, even with the big firms, they tell me that the training in their organization is definitely lacking, and that's why they come to someone like me. In addition to getting coaching for themselves, they definitely want to hear me interview people like you, too.

It's funny, Willy. There was a situation once where I knew somebody else who is a trainer in the industry, and he was doing a webinar for one of the major companies. He said, "Hey, Jim, I want to bring you on and interview you on this particular subject because I know you'd do a really good job."

Then he was laughing with me also, and he said, "You know, there's a broker who is with one of the other major companies that I really want to bring in on another webinar, and the company that has hired me to do the webinar said, 'Absolutely not. We don't want anybody from any of our competitors being interviewed on these webinars at all.'"

Then he and I were both chuckling. Wouldn't you love to have your competitors bare their soul about what they're doing that's making them money? Here the executive in charge is just saying, "No, we've got to keep it pure. We've got to keep the people being interviewed restricted to just being the people within our own company."

It's just so funny the way that sometimes the corporate people see it versus the salespeople who would probably say, "You'd bet I'd love to hear what my competitors are doing in running their businesses!"

We've talked about mailing and about the networking and the building of relationships and the things that you're doing. Are you doing much these days with marketing and staying in contact with your people with email?

Willy: Not too much. I'm sensitive to a couple of things, maybe overly sensitive because different people have different thoughts. I get 400 emails a day. I can't keep up with my emails. I have an assistant on Mondays, and his job is to delete 2,000 emails a week minimum. I can't go through everything.

The other thing that is more of a challenge is a lot of my emails go to my spam folder or my junk folder, and I miss a lot of them. I have to have someone double-check them, and it takes hours to go through that.

So I'm not doing a lot of emails because people are getting too many emails, and don't want to get them, and I don't get on email lists.

It's the same with correspondence. When I send something out, I want it to be important, not junk. I never send out jokes or any of that stuff. I respect people's time, and I want people to respect mine, too. So when I send something, they know it's important, and they read it as opposed to just getting a lot of stuff too often.

Jim: Sure, absolutely. You were talking about the spam you were getting. There was one email address I had, and I guess it's been about a year now, where I was getting 300 spam emails a day. So I cut it loose, and my life has been so much more relaxed since then. So now I've devised a different system of having a number of different email addresses. One is one that I tell people publicly, and that I email them from back and forth, and I have other ones that I sign up for free e-newsletters on, and another one for vendors that I do business with, and another one for friends.

I want to compartmentalize it, and the ones that are most likely to get the spam--the ones that I'm signing up for e-newsletters on and buying products with--I want to be able to cut that one email address loose and not have all these other accounts and relationships with people affected...and so far it's working out pretty good.

But I will tell you this. I've found that there is primarily one company that is sending me the majority of the spam. I mean, they've got every single email address I've got. They'll do it for several weeks, and then they'll disappear and I'll have no spam. Then they'll reappear again. I'm thinking that they're probably just getting shut down in different locations, and they find a new place in a different country, and then they're up and running again until they get shut down once more.

Gosh, it's tough trying to stay ahead of them and get them out of our hair, but we've got to do the best we can do...especially since I've got no more hair.

Willy: You were talking about prospecting. I want to mention a couple of funny stories about prospecting, as there is business everywhere to be had.

Two weeks ago my wife and I were at a store that sells security cameras for your house. I started talking to the owner of the company, and we just started talking and building rapport. I had mentioned that I had just done a deal in San Jacinto, which is a bedroom community. It was a tough deal to do, and I took it on because it was a relationship.

Jim: Yes, San Jacinto is about 20-30 minutes from me.

Willy: The guy goes, "You know San Jacinto? I've got five acres of commercial land. Would you like to sell it for me?"

I mean, out of the clear blue sky! I just told him what I do and that I had done a deal there. I didn't expect that. It was just like I was in a store, shopping with my wife for a product he was selling. I got into the conversation, and boom! He's giving me a listing if I want it.

Jim: That's great!

Willy: There are deals everywhere to be had. It's just a matter of getting engaged and talking with people. Before I was married for my second time, I joined a dating service called "It's Just Lunch". We've all heard about it.

Well, I joined the service. I paid my fee, and I started talking to them. They were in Newport Beach. All of a sudden they said, "Well, you're a broker. Could you help us relocate our office?"

I said, "Sure." So I relocated their office. My commission was three times what my fee was to them, and then, because I built a relationship, every time they had a new client, I got pick of the litter. I got introduced to more dates than I wanted, and it was unbelievable. It's just a matter of talking to them. There is business everywhere to be had. I can't tell you how many times I've been in stores talking to people and owners, and they said, "Hey, look, we need more space." Or, "We have too much space," and then you just take care of them.

There is business to be had. You just have to talk.

Jim: I'll tell you something else that's going on that is inherent in this. You have a presence about you that is very businesslike, very knowledgeable, very honest, sincere, and down-to-earth, and you seem like a solid person who has the answers and who can guide them in the right direction.

Somebody else could have come in and said the same thing about being a commercial broker, and the person might not have gotten that same feeling, and they wouldn't have mentioned anything about the land that they have or the requirement.

So that's a testimonial to who you are also, and how you make people feel in your presence. I'll give you a perfect example of this. Sometimes I have residential agents knock on my door at home. When I open the door, I'm evaluating whether or not I'd want to work with the person. It's just interesting observing that process in my mind, and realizing that in commercial, people are doing the exact same thing with you.

When you're prospecting on the phone, and when you're meeting with somebody face-to-face, they're evaluating everything about you, what you're saying, the tone of your voice, your body language, the feeling that you give them about you, and they're asking themselves, "Would I want to work with this person?"

They may have a requirement, but if something is wrong with your presentation that doesn't feel good or doesn't feel right to them, they may not even bring it up. In your situation, you exude confidence and that you care about people, and you exude professionalism, and you're down-to-earth at the same time, which is a tremendous bundle of qualities all within one person, and I believe that makes people more comfortable in telling you that they have a commercial real estate need.

I think that is also a testimonial to who you are and how you show up as a person, and as a broker in front of people.

Willy: Thank you.

Jim: So I just wanted to make that clear. You could have two different brokers canvassing a certain neighborhood or calling the exact same people over a two-to-four week period, and one of them is going to walk away with more leads because the principals felt more comfortable opening up about what their need was to that one broker over the other broker. That's where presentation skills come into play in a very huge way.

Looking down the road, how do you see commercial real estate brokerage changing? You talked a little about how things are changing, but in looking into your periscope down the road, or your crystal ball, what do you see in terms of where everything is now evolving and moving towards?

Willy: I mentioned earlier about the residential market going online and the commercial market going online. Every attorney who takes a client, the first thing they do is Google you. I recommend that you Google all your clients, and I recommend you Google yourself to see what's on the internet about you, because people are going to Google you.

Part of the internet is people have access to all kinds of information to be able to see product, and then they need help to do the transactions. So I think it's important that you have a good internet presence.

Every broker at the minimum should have a good LinkedIn profile. The advantage of LinkedIn is it's free, and it's one of the first things to pop up when you Google somebody. You control what is said about you, and you put everything in there. So I think everybody should Google themselves, everybody should be on LinkedIn, and it doesn't take any money or effort to do this.

Also regarding LinkedIn, I just attended an SIOR conference where there was a LinkedIn professional who said you have to make sure that you stand out and you say what you do and you ask for the business. These are concepts that I never considered about LinkedIn, but in LinkedIn, also join as many groups as you can. You can join up to 50 groups. Ask people to go on yours or go on theirs. I have over 2,000 people underneath me. I belong to 50 groups. Like everything, I'm not as active as I should be. I should be more active in the LinkedIn groups as they make comments or contribute. I just don't have time, but I'm trying to get this college intern to help me with some of that.

So in the future, you've got to be more visible on the internet. It's easy to do, and it doesn't have to cost a lot of money.

Also, more people are going to continue accessing products on the internet. LoopNet, which is great for mom and pops, and everybody should have their listings on LoopNet; it's free. If you pay for the better service, it's good, but not everybody has access to that.

Jim: We have a question coming from Brandon. Brandon please go ahead and state your question.

Brandon: I wanted to know some of the best ways to differentiate between a qualified prospect and a prospect who is wasting your time.

Jim: Willy, why don't you take that one first?

Willy: Ask a lot of questions. Find out if they have their capital ready to go, and find out what they really want. You find out pretty quick if you take them on a tour and they're asking serious questions, or if they're just getting a feel for the market.

Like I said earlier, all we have is our time and our knowledge and how we utilize it to determine how much money we make. Qualifying a prospective client is always a big issue. The rapport is always critical as well as the communication. Do they show up on time? Are they serious? Are they asking the right questions, or are they just tire-kicking? How long have they been searching? Are you the only broker they're working with? That's a big challenge. Are they only working with you, or are they working with everybody else? Where are they getting their information, and what is their need?

You just have to ask the questions to get a feel for it. Are they really serious? Why are they looking to do what they're doing? Are they investing, or are they going to relocate their company to lease or to buy? It's a challenging question.

Jim: Yes, and the exact types of questions you're going to ask depends on the type of prospect, and whether they're an owner looking to sell, a buyer looking to buy, a landlord looking to lease, or a tenant looking to lease on the tenant side.

Let's say, for example, it's a buyer or a lessee and they're saying, "We need 40,000 square feet to move into." One of the questions you could ask is, "Since the market is very tight right now, what's going to happen if you don't find this 40,000 square feet within the next six months?"

You want to hear an answer like, "Oh my gosh! That would be horrible because we're busting out at the seams and it's costing us money, and we need a better layout." That's the kind of stuff you want to hear as opposed to, "Well, if we don't find it in six months, it's really no big deal. We can pretty much stay where we're at right now. We've got a good landlord, and he'll let us stay month-to-month for as long as we want."

That last answer shows more of a lack in motivation. Similarly, let's say an owner is thinking of listing to sell. You could say something similar to, "What's going to happen if a year from now you still own this property?"

Then maybe they'll say, "Oh, we can't do that because we've got partners and everybody is at each other's throat. We've got to split the money, and we're all driving each other nuts." You want a sense that there is motivation as opposed to, "Well, if we don't sell in a year, it's no big deal. We're getting good rent from the tenant, and we just thought it would be kind of nice to sell. But in the end, if we're still getting income from it a year from now, that would be fine with us, too."

You have to ask questions like that. Learn what these questions are. Write them down so you have them around and you can ask them in different situations, depending on what type of principal you bump into and which question would be the most appropriate one to ask in the moment.

That's a very, very good question, Brandon.

Jim: We have another question from Rob.

Rob: First of all, thanks Willy. I really enjoyed the last hour and fifteen minutes. My question is for both of you, if you want to answer it also, Jim.

When you ask a buyer or a tenant for an exclusive authorization to represent and they ask you why they should do this, in your opinion, what are the top two reasons why that person should sign the exclusive authorization to represent agreement?

Willy: First of all, you want to make sure that you're the only broker representing them and you're not competing with a bunch of other brokers. You also want to say that if you're going to make a commitment, you need them to make a commitment with you also, because you're going to put a lot of time and effort into it.

It shows commitment on both sides, and agency laws are becoming very critical. That's another thing you could say. "I'm representing you, and nobody else."

Most lawsuits involving brokers or agents today are more related to agency laws than anything else, so that protects you. You can say, "This really documents who I'm representing and who I'm loyal to."

It's a commitment on both parts.

Jim: Sure, and basically you want to turn it around to them in terms of what's in it for them, because they may not care about what's in it for you... that you really want to become their exclusive broker. You've really got to think about this in terms of what's in it for them.

One of the things you could talk about is, "Have you ever in the past gotten sick and tired of all these different brokers wasting your time and submitting the same properties to you that you've already seen before?" For people who have been in business and have already made several moves, they could probably identify with something like that.

Let me mention something around this that can help to take this to another level. One of the things that can keep owners from signing an exclusive right to represent as a buyer or lessee can be the length and complexity of the form that you put right in front of them. It can be drafted by attorneys, and it can be lengthy. In addition, it can be scary.

One broker who I've coached did something that I thought was great. He basically developed a form that was just several sentences long--maybe just a couple of short paragraphs. It said something similar to, "Such-and-Such Company agrees that ABC Brokerage Company represents them exclusively for the procurement of ..." and then you describe what the requirement is. Then you say, "Such-and-Such Company will work exclusively through us, and they will refer any broker inquiries directly to us for follow-up." Then it says that this agreement will expire on whatever the expiration date is, but it can be cancelled at any time by either party by giving 30 days' advance written notice of the intention to do so to the other party.

So it looks and sounds fairly innocuous here, but it's easier for someone to sign this than a more detailed form. The beauty about this, though, is having the 30 days' advance written notice of cancellation in there. Let's say another broker then comes to them and says, "Hey, I've got the ideal building for you."

Your client says, "Oh my gosh! I've got this exclusive agreement. But wait a second, I can cancel it. But in 30 days the building will be gone and somebody else will have it by then. Can't you two brokers talk and then work something out between the two of you?"

So that 30 days' advance written notice can be huge in the moment, and I always recommend that you get legal advice on this. You just really want to have something where they're thinking, "What happens if I go behind their back and then close the deal with the other broker? What would I be liable for because I've signed this agreement?" That can be enough glue to want to keep you in the deal and find a way for everyone to work it out with the other broker.

So I would consider something like that, and then when you have the agreement with you and you're out to lunch with the person ahead of time, you could say, "Listen, let me give you an idea of how my business works. We don't get paid by the hour like CPAs and attorneys; we get paid on commission. That means that we have to be only working with people who will be loyal to us, who we know we're going to close a transaction with, and that we're going to get paid from it. If I work with somebody like you and then you end up closing a deal with another broker, I've lost all that time, and I can never get it back. That means money to me. So I want to work with you and I want to know that we can move forward together, because you're not one of those people who would ever want to do something like that and have me completely waste my time with you...would you?"

Then they'll say, "Oh, no. Absolutely not."

Then you say, "Great! This is why I have this really simple agreement so we can come together with this basic understanding, and it's cancellable by either one of us at any time with 30 days' advance notice." Then you show them the agreement.

So you're educating them, because I think many people don't believe that they're doing something wrong to a broker when they make a deal with another broker. They just think that it's a horse race, and this is how business works. So you educate them like that and let them know how you'll feel, and then you have a simple agreement which can help to set the tone and get a signature on it.

We have another question from Rob.

Rob: Now that you've mentioned that approach for dealing with a prospect, are you doing anything tomorrow at 2:00 p.m., Jim?

Jim: "Yes, I'm representing my client, Rob, here…"

Rob: That was great! I appreciate it.

Jim: We have another question from Brandon.

Brandon: Thank you very much. I have a quick question about starting out your career, and when you felt that you were making it. I'm in my first year going into my second. Sometimes it's kind of hard prospecting every day. When did you feel like you were starting to make it, like you'd really gotten going?

Willy: When you start making money, good money and good commissions, is when you start making it.

What you have to realize is you're building a practice. This is a profession. This is a career. It takes time to develop and evolve. One of the things you really need to do early on is figure out who you are and what you are, what your product type is, what your geographic area is, and become the local expert. Know every single deal, every single owner, every single tenant, and every single broker in that niche and that market, and then you'll really start to dominate a market.

Jim: There you go. Just keep putting one foot in front of the other, and keep doing the things that we're talking about here. Keep making your calls. The more calls you're making, ideally ten to twelve hours of prospecting a week, the more business you're going to be developing for yourself. Then you need to become an expert and a master at following up on the key leads and getting them enrolled in working with you exclusively, and then close the business.

It takes time, but just keep doing the right thing, and learn how to improve yourself constantly as a broker along the way.

As we're now moving towards completion, Willy, thank you so much for being on this call with us. I know you've got to go, and I told you I would get you out of here by the bottom half of the hour, and that's where we're at right now. Do you have anything that you'd like to say as we're wrapping-up and moving forward?

Willy: No, I've said a lot. I always have a lot more to say, but we're running out of time. I've enjoyed this call, and like always when you and I do this, one thought leads to another.

Jim: Absolutely. It creates a chain of a lot of other thoughts after I put the phone down from the call, too. I greatly appreciate you taking the time to do this. It's wonderful to know you, as the two of us have known each other over the years, and you're not only an exceptional broker, but you really care about teaching other brokers and giving back to the community.

There are a lot of brokers who I've called who flat-out say, "Why would I ever want to get on a call and tell people how I'm running my business?" So I greatly appreciate you taking the time to do this, my friend.

Willy: They say that if you really want to know something, you've got to teach it. When we do these calls, we prepare. I give a lot of lectures and talks to a lot of organizations, and I've contributed to articles and professional magazines, and it always comes back. The more you give, the more you get back.

Call it karma or give it to the universe. Whatever you want to call it, it will come back to you many times. Give first without the expectation of receiving, and it will come back to you. From my lectures to groups people say, "Hey, will you help me do this deal?" I can't tell you how many times I've spoken to people and they've approached me and said, "Help me do a deal and share a commission." Sharing a commission is better than no commission at all.

Jim: Yes, and I have people who are members of this program who listen to people like you talk. They'll see you speaking at a conference or something like that. They'll walk up to you and say, "I've heard you on Jim Gillespie's interviews. Thank you so much. The things that you said really helped me take my business to the next level." Or they may say something like, "I really aspire to be more like you." It's wonderful because you're talking to a number of people who are hearing you right now, but you don't know who they are or their names, and you haven't seen their faces. But it's nice to know that you're making an impact like this. People care about the fact that you've been willing to take the time to do this.

Again, I greatly appreciate you for that.

If you're ever interested in more detailed one-on-one coaching where we do 30-minute coaching calls two, three, or four times a month, let me know through my website at www.CommercialRealEstateCoach.com.

Thanks to everybody including Willy for being on the call today!

INTERVIEW 3

Making Powerful Presentations That Will Get You More Listings

Jim: Hi, this is Jim Gillespie, America's Premier Commercial Real Estate Coach^{sm} located on the web at www.CommercialRealEstateCoach.com. Today our teleconference is titled, "Making Powerful Presentations That Will Get You More Listings," and today I'm going to be interviewing our special guest, John DeGrinis, SIOR.

Here's my Introduction for John:

John DeGrinis, SIOR, has been with Colliers International for more than 25 years, and he's constantly been a leader within the Southern California commercial real estate market. Within the past seven years, John and his team have closed transactions totaling approximately 10 million square feet, representing $450 million in transaction volume.

In 2010, John received the award from SIOR for closing the largest dollar volume transaction of the entire year, featuring two buildings totaling more than 1.1 million square feet, which sold for more than 68 million dollars. John's clients over the years have included Rockefeller Group, Prologis, General Electric, NBC Universal, Lockheed Martin, Sears, and Toyota – so just a few small names there for me to drop, basically.

With that being said, please join me in welcoming onto our teleconference today John DeGrinis. John, I greatly appreciate you taking the time to be here with us.

John: I'm happy to join you today. Thanks for that great Introduction.

Jim: Yes, it's kind of nice to hear it back. You go, "Hey, that guy sounds pretty impressive, doesn't he?"

John: I don't know. It's hard to imagine that much time has passed and that all those years have gone by. I'm an old guy now.

Jim: And I'm sure even though you've got some great names of clients and companies you've represented, you go back and you probably had to grind it out with a few personalities that maybe weren't that pleasant along the way, too.

John: Oh my gosh! That is a part of every broker's life! Absolutely.

Jim: But at least the transactions closed with them, so you can at least say, "Hey, these people were represented by me," which is great.

John: Yes, it's always nice to have some of those marquee names as a part of your contact list.

Jim: And just so everybody knows, John and I are old friends. John and I are both Past Presidents of the AIR Commercial Real Estate Association, which is the prominent commercial real estate brokerage association in Greater Los Angeles, in Southern California, and I believe it may be the largest and most influential commercial real estate brokerage association in the Western United States. They really produce some amazing transaction forms.

If you're looking for great forms and addenda for your transactions, go check out their forms at www.AIRCRE.com. They're great, and they're constantly updated along with the input of people like escrow people, attorneys, and principals. It's really a wonderful organization.

John and I were both on the Board of Directors for many years together, and he's just such a great guy, a bright personality, and fun.

John: Yes, you get all sorts in every group.

Jim: You were always great to have, and bright with good ideas, and you were positive. It's great to finally have you here. I know we've chatted a couple of times over the years about doing this, but we finally were able to put it all together this time, so good.

John: Well I'm happy to be here.

Jim: Good. So, in your opinion, what do you think are the most important activities that brokers need to be doing, in order to produce great results in their brokerage businesses?

John: I think that there is probably one core competency that most brokers need to have, because as most of us realize who are in this business, it's not very often that the phone rings where someone will call and say, "Hey, I need a 100,000 square-foot building." It just doesn't happen as much as we would like, even in the go-go days when the market's been hot.

I would say prospecting--cold-calling if you will--is probably one of the core competencies that a broker needs to have to be successful. As I look at the company that I work for and the people that make up the upper echelon of producers, almost every one of them started off as a cold-caller. They were just dialing and smiling, or "dialing for dollars", however you want to look at it. I believe that this is really the trait that needs to be perfected as a broker.

Jim: When you talk about cold-calling, everything begins with cold-calling. There's actually a guy I've coached over the years, and he's got a sign that he puts on his desk that says, "Every transaction I've ever closed began with a cold-call." It's so true.

It's easy to begin to think, "I really don't need to make the calls; I'm so busy." Or, "I'd like to make the calls, but I'm just so busy." It's so important, because you know that when you drop out your cold-calling, somewhere down the road in your pipeline there's going to be holes in it, or you're going to be grabbing and holding onto people who are the more marginal clients to be working with.

John: You're exactly right, but I think there are some other things. I've done some speaking within my organization and I get asked, "What does it take to be successful?"

One of the things that I think cold-calling did for me, and I started off right out of college--very green, very eager, but at the same time very afraid of what was ahead of me. They said, "Here's a phone. Here are some 3x5 cards that we paid for. You go ahead and call them."

At first it's a daunting task. You're calling somebody that you don't know and you're having to make some sort of impression on them to where they're going to either a) give you some information, b) maybe meet with you, or c) if you hit the jackpot he may have a requirement that you actually can work on. But what you're trying to do is impress that individual so they give you more information which then leads you to the next steps of the entire sales process.

What I think that cold-calling does is it gives one a level of confidence to be able to open doors that would otherwise remain shut if you didn't pick up the phone, or actually go out in person and cold-call.

I think there was a period of time that I witnessed--and I can only speak for my company and maybe those that I work with at other companies--there was a time when everybody can remember the 2000's in our industry. There were the go-go days as I call them. There were deals happening. You could walk out in the middle of the street as they say and get hit by a speeding deal. I've heard that term used.

There were a lot of people making lots of money--these young individuals in the business--that were getting leads that were just handed over to them. "Here, run with this. Run with this." Some people could make quite a nice living doing that, but when the music stopped playing so to speak, they were ill-equipped to be able to go out and do what was necessary--and that was to pick up the phone and call people and try to get that information that would lead to the next step in the sales process.

I really believe that makes you a very, very competent individual and gives you the courage to do just about anything that's required in this business. There's more than just filling the pipeline, Jim.

Jim: When you talked about the days when everything was on fire and everything was going great, I remember once I went out to one of our dinner events for the AIR Commercial Real Estate Association that I've mentioned. The market was on fire, and one of the guys getting up and giving a presentation about his market said, "You want to know how on fire this market is? Do you really want to know?" Then he refers to a client he's been working with who's from a country that, shall we say, is really known for people negotiating and grinding you down on every last nickel. He says, "The market is so on fire that I showed a guy from this country a building and he asked me what the asking price was...and I told him. Then he looked at me and said, 'Let's offer full price'. That's how on fire this market is!"

In addition, John, something about prospecting that I've found very fascinating, not only with myself as a broker but with the people who I've coached, is that the biggest problem with brokers not doing their prospecting is resisting the thought of how horrible and uncomfortable they think it's going to be, while they're not doing it.

The crazy thing is that when you pick up the phone and you start dialing for about 15 minutes or so, all of a sudden it starts to feel OK, and maybe even good, you know?

John: I absolutely agree. I think once you get into a rhythm, it becomes much better. We have one individual on our team who just loves it. The thrill of prospecting is something that really drives him.

Now I look at this as definitely being a requirement of the business, but I can't say I love it. It's very, very fulfilling when you're able to make contact with somebody that you've tried to talk to for a long time, and then you actually get some good information, and then get a meeting. Those are little wins along the way that win the overall war, if you will. It's something that is required, and you're right. After you get into a groove, you can be quite effective at it.

The other thing is I'm a firm believer in scripts. Look, you can make a script where you're getting four or five points across to this individual in a pretty short period of time. Otherwise you're going to lose his interest. Those 20 seconds of words need to be impactful. If you figure out something that works for you, there's no reason why you shouldn't keep using it.

Then, of course, you can move and adapt and pace and mirror based on what kind of conversation you're having, but once you get that guy on the phone, you want to make sure at least in the first few seconds that you've demonstrated a) a level of competence, b) a level of energy, and c) maybe some information that might be relevant to him.

Again, I think there are a lot of things going on, but once you get into a rhythm it kind of flows, and it can actually be kind of fun.

Jim: I think there are several different goals that brokers can have within the prospecting and calling process. I think a really important one is you want to make sure that when the decision maker gets on the line, that you get them to want to engage in a conversation with you, so that now they're sort of relaxed and thinking, "It's OK for you to ask me questions now and for me to answer," instead of you constantly being in that place where you're just hoping they don't want to hang up the phone on you.

John: Agreed.

Jim: There are ways to do that, and I discuss them in detail when I interview my guest experts on prospecting. It's just so important, because you want to have them say, "Yes, please tell me about that building you're calling me about." Or, "Yes, please tell me about what's going on in the marketplace. I want to know." This is a very important first step.

John: I'll add to that one little thing.

Jim: Please.

John: I think that when you engage that person on the phone, I remember when I was first doing it. It seems like my tonsils would rise up into my mouth and I'd get all choked up because I was talking to the facilities guy of a big company, or to the CEO. What's important is that you have to make sure, as you said, to be somewhat engaging and have some energy.

Oftentimes, I get cold-called by people and I get varying calls. I get the ones where they're literally reading from a script and they just don't sound interesting. My first thought is, "I don't want to talk to this person." Then you get the opposite, where they're engaging and you go, "You know what? I'm just going to play this one out." Then they get a lot of information out of me.

It's important to remember that we're all human. This person on the other end of the line wants to engage with a human being, if he's going to continue on with the discussion at all.

Jim: Since we're talking about presentations tonight, this definitely falls within the presentation category of how good you are at doing your prospecting and sounding natural at it, and having the other person want to engage in a dialogue with you is all about your presentation style, which the better you get at it, the more effective you're going to be at doing your prospecting.

John: Yep.

Jim: Good. So how receptive in general are you seeing brokers being towards changing their old routines, and doing what will have them begin producing better results in their brokerage businesses?

John: Well, years ago when we started cold calling we dealt with 3x5 cards with possibly a business card stapled to it, and then all the information about when you called them and what you mailed to them was scribbled into the smallest of script on that.

Obviously we've evolved now into computers and contact managers that make it quite easy to follow up, to stay in touch with the information, to follow up on the call that you're supposed to make, but there's no substitute for just doing it. That's one of the things. You can have all this technology available at your fingertips, but there's no substitute for just picking up the phone.

A lot of times I'll see younger brokers. They think they're working. They're seeing email, they're doing things on the internet, and that's not necessarily productive time.

But back to your question. Old dogs, when I got in the business, had a lot of hard times transitioning into the digital age. Many of the folks that were old, I'll call them "old", at the time that I got in the business are out of the business, and those who are still in it are the ones who made the transition to digitalization if you will, and are utilizing the tools that make our job a lot easier than it was.

Imagine life without email, or going back many years without having fax capabilities. We used to have to get stuff signed in person in those days and then hand-deliver it.

Our job has gotten a lot easier with technology. Some that weren't embracing it had a difficult time of surviving. There are a lot of other examples including tenant demands or client demands on being accessible. Obviously the smartphone has done a lot to keep us tethered to the information, or to a client's requirement to speak to us. Twenty years ago, once you left the office, that was pretty much it. There wasn't much interaction with your clients beyond that.

A lot of things that the clients have demanded have really formed what brokers' traits are. Another one is that a lot of the time we saw solo brokers, if you will, where one broker was responsible for his own world and his clients. That was it. Well, clients demanded more service and they wanted to have people who were teamed up. Obviously over the last 15 years we've seen a lot of teaming up going on for the reasons that I've mentioned.

If you don't adapt, you have the chance of maybe being left by the wayside. On the other hand, if you have such a strong business, you can weather a lot of storms by having a good clientele, but I don't know that there's a way to not adapt to the changing environment that we see going on year-to-year.

Jim: And I remember, and I've said this on some of these calls over the years, that back in 1990 I was the first person that I knew of in my territory to have a computer with contact management software. The old guys around the office, and even the younger guys who weren't into it yet, were showing me their business cards with the rubber bands around them and their index cards with the rubber bands around them saying, "Why do you need a computer? This works fine for us."

John: I know.

Jim: Imagine being without that contact management software now.

John: Or without email. A lot of people were very resistant to email, and we all know what that did to the industry, and to the whole business world.

Jim: So the subject of our call tonight is presentations. Keeping that in mind, how important do you think it is for brokers to have solid presentation skills?

John: Well, I like to look at presentations a little bit differently. There are always the formal types. I can elaborate on that a little bit later, but there are also the informal presentations. I think that one of the things that I've learned, because I've taken a lot of training, both from the company and outside, and one of the things that we're constantly reminded of is that your audience oftentimes doesn't remember what you said, but they remember how you said it, and how they felt when you said it.

The first thing is informal presentation. Let's say that you're cold-calling in person. This happens a lot, I think. You're banging on doors and you actually get somebody to say, "Yes, come in and talk to me."

He's making an assessment right then and there of what he views you as. What kind of skills do you have? What kind of verbal communication skills? Are you engaging? Are you someone that he likes? Above that, are you somebody that he likes that actually has a market presence? Are you valuable to him in the way of providing information in your role as a real estate broker?

I believe that when we're in front of a client, we're always presenting. It may not be formal, but it's informal. The way you carry yourself, the way that you live your business life in terms of in front of the client, I believe this is presentation in and of itself. There is a lot that goes into that.

Then of course there's the infamous pitch. That's where it gets interesting. What do they want to hear? What do they want to know? Oftentimes, and I'll speak for myself in the early days, I would just load that book up with every possible bit of information that I thought he would want to see. You've got this book that's about three inches tall with comps and data and things about me and articles and stuff about the building or the project. It's completely inundated.

Looking at it now as a businessman, who's going to read that? Well, I somehow felt that they would.

Jim: Yes, let's also put the scores of the current baseball games in progress in there, too!

John: It just doesn't work that way. Really, when you present, I believe that one of the first steps, and this is one of the things that we struggle with all the time, is to try to get that pre-meeting. What do they actually want to know? What is their circumstance? One of the things that has really changed our focus on my team is, and you hear it and it sounds so trite and so over-used, is what is the client's need, and being client-focused and client-centric. A lot of times we go in there assuming we know what they want, but we have no idea of what's driving a possible decision to list the building, because that's what they called you about, and trying to understand what are their underlying reasons, which is where all the gold is.

I strongly believe that you need to get that pre-meeting where you sit down and say, "Look, I'm going to take a half an hour. I really want to understand what is driving your interest in whatever the situation might be." Try to get in. It won't come out in the first few sentences in their answer. You'll have to dig and dig for it.

A lot of times we'll use this line, "If there was one last thing, what would it be?" A lot of times it's then and only then that you'll really get the juicy information.

"Well, my wife and I are getting a divorce and we're going to need to do something with the asset." You just wouldn't know that.

A lot of times these scenarios that you're taking for granted are just not the facts. As a result I believe that presentations oftentimes are won in the question and answer session that precedes the actual presentation.

Jim: That's extremely important information, because when you get to that point, like what you said when the guy says, "My wife and I are getting a divorce," there's a certain amount of emotional release and tension that comes out when he or she is saying what's going on with their marriage.

Now they've gone to a deeper level of bonding with you because they've now included that arena of their own personal life with you, whereas with other brokers they may have not wanted to go there.

You bring up a very solid point. Sometimes I'll hear brokers say, "What do I gotta do to get these owners motivated to sell?" People sell because of having to fulfill certain needs in their life because things are changing. Divorce is one reason. The desire to want to get out of one kind of property and into another one is another reason. Estate planning and needing to divide up the assets, splitting up from a partnership, these are other reasons.

It used to be that when the market was on fire and prices were going up and up and up all the time, greed was a good motivator. It was like, "OK, people, my building's only worth a million dollars, but if you can get me a million and one hundred thousand for it, I'll sell it." Then three months later the market takes off, they feel like they've made out like a bandit because you got them a million-one for it, and it's only because the market was taking off. They thought that they were really getting paid higher than the true market value for it.

John: I just think that, again, if you've got four brokers coming in to pitch, they're all going to have the same comps. They're all going to have the same availabilities. Who's going to win the business? Well, obviously there's a bit of salesmanship, I'll just use that term. The assignment can oftentimes go to the person who seems to have the personality that identifies well with the other individual, which is another thing that the pre-meeting does. It determines your decision maker and what type of individual he is, because one of the things that we've learned at Colliers is that there are four different types of people that you can throw into a category.

I'll just use generic terms. You've got the hardcore leader. We call them "control". They're focused, they're strong-willed, they make decisions, they're very decisive, and they want direct answers to direct questions. If you sit there and this guy asks you, "Well what is it going to take to move my building?", and you start talking about process and this and that and whatever, you're going to lose him as opposed to the accountant type. I think everyone can picture the accountant type. He's very rational, very orderly, he likes facts and figures to back up decisions, and he would probably react a little bit differently to the answer you would give the guy I just mentioned before.

He wants to know, "Here's what I think and here's why I think it and here's what I suggest," whereas the control guy, the hardcore leader if you will, wants quick, direct answers. He's going to size you up in the way you say it. He may look at the information you leave behind, or he may ask questions about why or what, but you've got to know your audience. If you're telling one guy a process that he's not really receptive to, or vice-versa, you've already made one kind of an impression on him.

Again, the pre-meeting I believe does so many things in addition to uncovering the real reason that someone is having you in that room with them, but it also tells you who your audience is and how you're going to structure your presentation towards them. If you're going to be long-winded, you're going to lose that hardcore leader type, and you will probably not get the business. That's another critical thing that you get out of having a pre-meeting.

For so many of us over the years we would just say, "OK, great." You put together the book and assume everything you believe they want. You go in there with your PowerPoint presentation and you'll bore them to tears, whereas in the pre-meeting you will determine a lot of those answers and know what not to do for the most part, and maybe you'll know a lot more than your competitors will, and your presentation will address their needs which, in the end, is what you're really trying to do.

Jim: This is great information, because so many brokers don't have a pre-meeting, and they go in there with the same canned presentation that they make to everybody, but they change the address of the building and the features of the building. When you go into a pre-meeting situation like that, you can do exactly what you've talked about and then ask certain questions like, "What's going to differentiate the broker who'll you'll give the listing to from everybody else?"

"What are the important questions that you want addressed during our listing presentation? Because it's important to us to make sure we provide you the answers to these important questions?" Then you can customize your presentation to address exactly what they said they want, and go in there hitting on all of the cylinders that are important to them. Whereas your competitors are going in there just with the same canned speech they give to everybody, and it just sounds so generic to the owner.

John: The other thing that you're able to do in a pre-meeting, because many of us don't do it, is you're able to get some of the other stuff out of the way. For example, you can subtly leave behind information. One of the things I like to say is, "Look, Mr. So-and-So, obviously you've invited us here because you felt that we had some sort of relevancy to the assignment, and I'd like to share with you the information that you might be interested in knowing about the transactions that we've previously been involved with. Here are a couple of case studies."

What that a lot of times allows you to do is get the opportunity to not have to deal with that in the presentation, because you've already earned the right to talk about his needs and not to focus on how great Colliers International is, or CB, or whoever you work for, and you get that out of the way.

So many times in my earlier years I'd go in there. You'd have this anxiety about making sure he knows all these deals that you've done, whether they're relevant or not. "I did this big deal and I did that big deal." He doesn't want to hear that. Generally speaking, if you've made the cut to sit down with him, he knows you have the ability. What's really going to resonate with him is your understanding of his problem and the alternatives that you've laid out to possibly address those problems with a potential solution that can show him where the gold is at the end of the rainbow.

Again, the pre-meeting I believe is where so many of the presentations are won. It took me many, many years to realize that.

Jim: I know that in this dialogue that we're having you've primarily been mentioning the decision maker as being a man. Of course we know that there are women in decision-making situations in commercial real estate, too.

John: How sexist of me! That is terrible.

Jim: I want to share a story that my long-time members will probably remember. It involves a hugely successful broker with 30+ years in the business, who's been with one of the major companies for over 20 years, a great guy, and he'll be listening to this interview, and he knows who he is. I remember years ago when I had a coaching call with him he was just scratching his head going, "Jim, I don't know what happened. I thought for sure we had the inside track with this company to get this listing on this big office building. But right at the last second they said, 'I'm sorry. You didn't get it.'"

He said that the person who was the team leader for the company's real estate committee was a woman. So he said to her, "I don't understand. I felt that we had the inside track. What is it that had you give the listing to the other people?"

Then she sternly said to him on the telephone, "They had a woman on their team, and you did not."

So I said to the broker, "Do you realize the huge gift that she just gave you by saying that?"

Then immediately he began interviewing people, and brought a woman onto his team.

John: You know, you can't always do that, but I would say that 20-25% of the people who we present to in a leadership role as the decision maker are now women. That's probably very different from when I got in the business 27 years ago, or whenever that was.

I mean no disrespect; I was just picturing a person that was a male in my little discussion there.

Jim: I understand, but I'm just saying nowadays, especially when committees are involved, you just never know what's being communicated behind the scenes with an agenda if somebody is angry about something like that. So rather than potentially be at the effect of it, why not, if you don't already have a woman on your team, consider having somebody on your team who's a great woman?

John: Absolutely.

Jim: I just wanted to mention that just for people out there who have teams, and for people who are thinking of putting together teams. Again, we're talking about presentation skills, and yet I find that there is so little training or focus, generally speaking, within the brokerage companies on how brokers need to deliver outstanding presentations, and on what they have to do to improve their presentations. Is this something you've noticed also? And if so, why do you think they've dropped this out and don't pay much attention to it?

John: Well, training brokers is a challenging thing. I used to be a selling manager for our profit center up here in the North Los Angeles region, so I was responsible for hiring people and I always had to have somebody with me, training them to be a broker within this office. Some of the things that really come into play is that training is extremely expensive, both from the standpoint of money and time, time really being where I think I spent most of my elements in.

If you really are going to be effective with somebody and get them to understand the business and to do it the "right way" if you will, you've got to spend a lot of time with them. That was one of the things that I realized early on. I've done that with my younger teammates. They've been with me for a long time now, but it all started out with really spending time and having them hear my conversations and asking them, "Look, if you hear any conversation, just walk in. Then afterwards you can ask me to explain what happened."

I believe that, sure, you can learn through experience, but I believe that you can flatten that learning curve a bit by having them be part of, or by listening to circumstances that we as brokers go through every day, and they will be able to shorten their learning period, at least for the most basic elements of the business, quite quickly.

The other thing is that we have a very high dropout rate in our industry. I mean, a lot of people get into this business because it's very lucrative, it's a very people-oriented business, and people like that, but it's a very competitive business. As a result of that, failure can be quite high in the industry for those who aren't determined to make it.

You train and spend so much time with people and then all of a sudden they bail. It's a difficult scenario to reconcile with sometimes, but you just have to keep doing it if you're going to create a cadre of people that you want to work with.

The last item is that in the old school most of the time, rather than in the new school, a lot of people were feeling that they were training their "runners"...because a lot of time that was the designation given to somebody young, a "trainee" if you will. You were training them to be your competitor, so a lot of guys looked at that as being counterproductive, so you didn't have successful brokers wanting to train younger brokers, and they would leave it to the company to do whatever training needed to be done.

I think you need a complement of having Jim Gillespie training you, but I also think that you have to have somebody who's there day-to-day guiding your move on every little thing that goes on. That's why I think the team concept that I've created, at least in my little world, I'm very proud of because I've created a scenario where I've got young guys who are all incentivized to do the same thing, to work hard for a collective goal where everybody is a part of that dollar income that comes in some way, shape, or form.

I view it as I'm training my partners. That isn't always the case, but I think that many of us look at training somebody now as training somebody that they want to grow with as opposed to just seeing them become another spinoff, and have them literally become another competitor in the office.

Jim: I kind of joke with people sometimes and I say, "You know, it's amazing when you talk to executives with companies and with their managers about training, and you pretty much across the board get statements like, 'Training is so important. Training is vital.' But then I find that in reality they don't want to spend much money on training." It's theory versus reality basically.

John: No doubt.

Jim: There's a guy who I've coached and who I've interviewed on these calls at different times over the years. He's a wonderful guy, a top producing SIOR member out of Houston, Texas named Mike Spears. Mike is the managing broker of his office down there, and something that they've done, which I think is great, is he'll go around to the different senior members in the office and basically enroll them in leading a presentation on a particular subject of excellence in commercial real estate, so he'll be rotating among these senior brokers throughout the months during the year.

Once a month or so, one of the guys will step up and lead his presentation on prospecting or on marketing or presentations, so he's getting participation from the great knowledge and wisdom of the other senior brokers in the office, but he's not dumping a ton of stuff on their shoulders at the same time.

If they're willing to step up for one or two presentations a year, he can spread it among the senior brokers, and it just works great for the office at the same time.

John: Yes, I think that's a great idea. We used to have that at our company, where we'd have people come together and teach the younger guys, and each guy would be responsible for a different aspect of things. They would offer their perspective on how to cold-call or how to time manage or how to do this or that.

That's a great way of doing it without having it be "formalized", where the people listening in on that presentation can really understand some tricks of the trade from that individual, and you get a lot of different people involved in offering their tricks of the trade. That is a great way of doing it.

Jim: We've talked a bit about presentations. You've talked about the pre-meeting also. Basically, if you were to sum it up as easily as you can, what do you think it is that differentiates the brokers who make outstanding presentations from everyone else?

John: You know, being the presenter so many times more than being the presentee, if I can use that term, we've asked our clients, "Why us? What compelled you to hire us? Because there were four other groups there." I want to know, and I don't get to ask that question that often, but a lot of times people have mentioned things like, "Well, you seemed believable. You seemed down to a human level. You addressed our needs. You really got into what was driving our situation as opposed to telling us about all the deals you have done."

We hear this comment often, "All we heard about is how great they were and how big this is, and nobody really focused in on what our driving goals were going to be." I think that one of the things that really changed the way that I approached this business was, again, it's to use that tired old thing, to be more client-centric. That means to really understand the client's goals. If you go to a doctor to diagnose your health situation, you don't want to hear him telling you about all the different procedures he's done here and there to try to convince you that he's a good doctor. You really are already there because he's a good doctor, or at least you perceive him to be, and you want him to tell you what your situation is.

I think that's the way we've looked at our business, at least from presenting to clients, both landlords and tenants, in trying to get to understand their needs and addressing those needs, because a lot of times they've already sized you up. I believe there's a certain swagger that comes along with not really beating on your own chest. Sure, I've got 25 years of experience and a lot of transaction volume, but I've seen younger people do the same thing without a big laundry list of transactions that they've done in the past, and they have gotten business that's surprising. You're thinking, "How did they get that?"

"Well, I just focused on what they needed and what they were looking to do, and focused my presentation on that."

The other thing is, look, let's face it, there are people who can execute quite well and there are probably many in the group that can do that, but then there comes this intangible. In this case, we're talking about an intangible within brokerage professionals. "How did he make me feel?" I believe that's another thing I've learned; people are human. People are wanting to hire the best service provider they can, all things being equal, but I think in the end they also place a pretty heavy importance on who they like, and I think sometimes we forget that. Being genuine, not being canned and sounding that way, because we all can see a canned presentation, and we can identify it. Someone says it's like porn, you know it when you see it, and you can identify it.

Again, I think by being genuine and addressing the client's needs, I think that's one of the things that we look at as our secret sauce.

Jim: Let's say we've got somebody listening who says, "OK, you've kind of stirred up the pot and got me thinking about some things, and I probably should take a look at improving my presentations." What recommendations do you have for anyone listening who would like to improve their presentation skills in terms of assessing what needs to be improved first, and then going about improving their presentation skills, so they then take them to the next level?

John: Now we're getting into the mechanics. A lot of time has been spent by our team in being trained mechanically. We've talked a little bit about being client-focused, but in the end you're going to have to go up there and give a presentation. Not all of them will be sitting across the table and doing it in an informal way. A lot of times you will be in front of a group and you will be presenting in the more formal meaning of the word.

One of the things that you've got to do is, we've got a pitch book that we've created from scratch. It addresses the way that we like to solve problems. A lot of times on the tenant side we'll focus on their current reality as we define it. We talk about what they're in, and then we get into their desired reality. This talks about what the goal is. Then from there we will go into the challenges and the opportunities of that, and then we'll talk about relevant case studies that might be similar to their situation, so that we can tell a story about how we handled another scenario like this. It's a way of bragging, but not really bragging, because you're basically getting them to understand the client that you've done business with prior, and how you've solved their problems. So to the extent that you can do that, it obviously helps.

There's no substitute for practicing it, planning it, and performing it. The other thing is, I'm the first to admit that I'm not a great public speaker. I do not feel comfortable in front of a large group, but I do it and I have trained myself to set aside that fear. I think most of us have a fear of public speaking. Some are gifted and don't have a fear of it, but most of us do. The only way to really overcome that is to do it, and when you avoid those scenarios it's just going to create a weakness that you will have a hard time getting over.

I'm constantly challenging myself to do that, because in the end, after you get into your groove like we talked about with cold-calling, it just flows, because you're getting into delivering the stuff you already know.

Again, planning, practicing, and performing, and knowing your presentation well is really important. The other thing is that sometimes we get caught up in trying to get too much information out there, and that relates to the pre-meeting and focusing your message on what their needs are going to be. If you can focus on that, a lot of times you'll find that you can achieve the points of discussion that you knew you wanted to go over.

A lot of times you may not go in the exact order you want because presentations oftentimes end up going in different directions, but if you can just practice it over and over again, because presentations are made up of sound bites that you've rehearsed over and over again, that's information that your client wants to hear. If you deliver them over and over again, you will be well versed in how to say it and then say it in a way like I said before, that's human, that's believable, and that's genuine. I think being a genuine individual is one of the elements intangibly that people make decisions by, that they won't necessarily tell you.

Jim: People are crying out to experience salespeople who are genuine, and unfortunately, when people become salespeople, they oftentimes go to a place in their mind where they have this image of what they've heard salespeople are supposed to be like, and that then throws them into the canned presentation style, which is what bad salespeople do.

It doesn't have to be that way. I mean wouldn't most of us want to experience a salesperson who we felt truly cared about our needs above and beyond making a sale? Wouldn't we want to have somebody who's authentic, who we feel really connects with us instead of just metaphorically pushing a button and out comes this canned sales presentation, which really serves to keep the distance between the salesperson and the prospect they're trying to enroll in doing business with them?

John: Right.

Jim: That's what we want.

John: What you just said, Jim, again, I've been around and I've seen a lot of different people tell us about what winning presentations are, and I've been around people internal to my company who have seen hundreds of presentations, and the one thing that keeps coming back is what you just said. It's having somebody who demonstrates a genuine interest in solving the client's problem. That is what we understand and what we hear over and over again as the difference between being an "also ran" and someone who gets the business.

It's huge. It's something, again, that I didn't know until later on. A lot of times we "show up and throw up" as they say. We leave a giant book of information, and maybe I demonstrated enough expertise on their general problem that they thought, "Yeah, he's better than the next guy. Let's go ahead and hire them." But throw out a lot of the chance scenarios to where I didn't address the client's needs, and we just didn't want to leave it all to chance.

What we've learned is that with everything else that we've talked about, if you can focus in on the client's needs, and then in a way weave in your own experience of helping the other companies out in similar scenarios, this gives the client the comfort level they want to have. "Has he done this before? Does he have experience?" That's another element of it. You can't just go in there and wow them and not have any experience in the task that you're telling them you can do.

Let's be truthful about it. You've got to have some experience. On the other hand, no one wants to hear all about what you've done. They want to have a combination of, "This guy's got experience. He's shown me similar scenarios of how he's helped other companies like me. The guy seems genuine. He does this task and that task. He likes that hobby and this hobby."

One of the other things I failed to mention is establishing some level of rapport if you can. A lot of times that can be done in the pre-meeting where you see something on the guy's credenza. You see that he's a basketball fan. You brush up on your knowledge of NBA basketball or on hockey, or whatever.

Getting a commonality is a huge, huge barrier breaker. That's something that you can read about in any sales book, but it applies. Again, there are a lot of different aspects that go into presentations including what I call "salesmanship". That means being an intent listener, and not talking as much as you are listening. Really, where you're going to gain all the gold is when he's talking, not when you are.

Jim: We've all heard people say, "You talk too much," but have you ever had anybody say, "You listen too much?"

John: That's rare.

Jim: In terms of building that rapport, something that can be helpful sometimes, too, is when you're in the person's office, just look around at the kinds of things they have on their walls. If they have photos of themselves golfing or playing tennis or doing something with the Boy Scouts or whatever, this can give you some insight into where their love and their passion is outside of work. If you can go to a place and talk to them about that or share a common experience, that can be a wonderful way to build that bond and rapport. Whereas if you don't look around the office or on the walls, or on their desk, you're sort of just shooting blanks, not knowing, and just guessing.

That information about what they have decorating their office can really help you immensely to know where their passion is, that you can then really connect with.

John: Some types are a little bit more robotic, but most people aren't robots, and they want to know that the person who they're dealing with is human on the other end, and that they do similar activities. If you can identify a commonality between you and the person you're presenting to, it's huge. Then you get to talking about that.

There's a gentleman by the name of Max Green who was one of the people that pushed our company, The Seeley Company as it used to be called, to the next level.

Jim: I remember that name.

John: Max was known to be one of those kinds of guys who would walk into someone's office, and they would talk about everything other than real estate. Then it was an, "Oh, by the way..." and he would get business most of the time using that approach. Now, not all of us are that gifted, or maybe it was a different era, but again, the personal nature of who we are as human beings, as people, is a very important part of making presentations in my world, because I think that people don't dismiss the fact that they really want to work with people who they like.

Jim: Sure, absolutely, and people ideally want to work with people who they consider to be their friends. If you can establish that friendship relationship instead of just an arm's length business transaction relationship, that's the kind of relationship that is a "friends" relationship that will lead to repeat business, because it's very hard for people to stop doing business with people they consider to be their friends. It's very easy to stop doing business with somebody they close a transaction with that they didn't really build a friendship with, because other brokers will constantly be calling them. It's then easy to build that relationship with other brokers before their next transaction. But with friends, when you have that ongoing relationship in place with them, it's very difficult for them to then work with another broker instead of you, because you've now become their friend.

John: Yes, it's a bond. One of the other key things that we started doing, and it seems stupid to not know this, is asking these clients who you've done well for and who like you, "Do you know of anybody else that I might be able to assist in their real estate needs?"

It's amazing how many times you will be recommended to someone. You just ask the client, "Is there anybody else that I might be able to help?"

"Yes, I was talking to so-and-so at a cocktail party, and I told them you did this. I gave him your name, but…" Then a lot of times that may be where it ends. So make sure you ask your client for that information so you can follow-up directly with the other person.

"Yes, I was telling Bill of So-and-So Company, and you should call him."

Again, it's something that you want to remember. That personal touch and that personal bond a lot of times is gold.

Jim: Something that I tell people to do that basically takes what you've just done there and builds on it a little bit is, before you ask them for the referral, maybe you'll be sitting down someplace where ideally they're not getting interrupted, or maybe you're out to lunch with them or in a quiet environment. Then you can say something similar to, "Bob, I love working with you. You're someone who's a good friend and I greatly value our relationship together. So I have a question to ask you and here it is: Who do you know who may be looking to buy, sell, or lease commercial real estate?"

When you give them that heartfelt compliment in advance, and you want it to be a genuine compliment, it helps to put them in the place where they're thinking, "They just made me feel really nice about both me and our relationship together. Now I want to think of someone I can refer them to."

John: We've spent a lot of time talking about the personal, human part of it all, but sometimes we deal with the classic accountant-type who doesn't crack a smile for much. He's pretty much all business. He doesn't want to talk about small talk. Maybe that's all he does is look at numbers all the time.

We work well with those types as well because we're able to identify them and we're able to speak to them in a manner that they are receptive to hearing. Again, with a person like that, you don't want to talk about fluff; you want to deal with facts, figures, and assessments based on those facts and figures, because that's how they look at it.

Those types of individuals need to be sold in a different way, to use a very trite term. In the same way, they can be very impressed with what you're doing for them, and they are a source of additional opportunity as well. It's not just the guy that you're all warm and fuzzy with. It can also be those who you've done good work for. Again, we have all types who occupy the business world, men, women, accountant-types, influence-types, all of them will have their own traits and characteristics.

Jim: We've been talking about presentations and presentation styles, and how people can improve their presentations. Describe for us your listing presentation package, the package that you give to people. Sometimes people in our industry call it the "leave behind" because you leave the package there and they can kind of thumb through it whenever they want to. How big is your presentation package, generally speaking, and what kinds of things do you include in it?

John: We spent probably six years getting it to where it is right now. We had someone professionally from within the company come and help us with what our message was. Let me start by saying that before it used to be a lot of boilerplate, a lot of text, a lot of data, a lot of this and that. It had stuff that I wouldn't want to read. It took me a long time to realize that my clients didn't want to read it either. I thought that they might want to read it, but they don't.

So you come in with a big book and it's kind of hard to really go over that book with them, because you've got an inch-thick package. "Turn to page 22," and then they're looking on page 30. You've lost control, and your message is going to be diluted.

What we've done is we've really tried to focus in on the client's need. If we're able to get that pre-meeting, we will understand their current reality. The first page of our book is really the current reality. I'm looking at one right now. "You own a 50,000 square foot good-quality industrial building. It's leased to this company until January of next year. They're paying this amount." So it identifies the parameters that exist.

Then you get into the desired reality. They want to sell the property, but the value is so low because you've got a tenant in there who has a short-term lease, along with very short notice options. It's very difficult to maximize the overall value.

We establish those scenarios. Then we go into the property and we discuss the property. We discuss the challenges of the property. It's not tall enough, it doesn't have enough loading, there's deferred maintenance, there's this, and there's that. Then you get into the opportunities, the positives, and all the elements that deal with this that owners would pay the most for. Perhaps the tenant can be induced to move out, etcetera. You have a little bit of information about the building like an aerial, or whatever other information might be relevant.

Again, you're not trying to create a fat book. You're trying to deal with information that you're actually going to be going over with the client.

We print it out in 11x17 format. We walk with the client through this presentation. You don't read everything. We'll touch on things that are relevant, and it usually spurs a significant amount of discussion, which is the kind of meeting that I like, anyhow, so that we have more of an interactive discussion as opposed to me just babbling.

There are a few things with respect to relevant lease or sale data that would be important to any discussion, particularly on a listing pitch. Maybe we'll go over a few relevant alternatives in the marketplace, basically the competition. Again, depending on what their focus is, we can tailor the presentation that way.

In this particular one, they were very concerned about the valuations given, since they had an existing lease which created a value of x, and if the building were vacant it created a value of x plus 20%. We spent a lot of time looking at that data because we knew that it was important to them. They were less interested about who our company was, and they were less interested in our long list of clients.

Another page deals with a review of the process; What happens when they engage us, what we're going to do with the existing tenant, how we're going to posture them, what we're going to do in the way of marketing, because in this case we were not going to go widespread because it was not going to be that kind of an offering. We had the "if/then" scenarios. Everything was kind of a flow chart, if you will, that is very easy to read.

Again, we went over all of this with them. Then maybe you have a couple of case studies that you can share and talk about how you did this for a similar scenario, and what the results were. Then we'd talk about who our marketing audience is, who is the target market, who are we focused in on, and who are maybe the second ring of potential targets, and the third ring.

Then we talk about our marketing process, which helps us deal with awareness and then understanding, interaction, and then ultimately a transaction. We just walk them through all that. Then sometimes they want to know what kind of marketing materials we use, and if we'll have a website, and everything in between.

We really try to get the information that they'll want to know about in the pre-meeting. Otherwise you don't know where to focus your time. Usually a presentation is an hour, maybe an hour and a half for a big property, or for one that deserves that kind of focus. You could be talking about stuff that they have no interest in. Again, the pre-meeting is so important.

Jim: Exactly. I was just thinking of that before you even brought up the subject of the pre-meeting again. I'm thinking that's where you address that and get that stuff out of the way, so you don't waste their time and they're thinking, "Why are they talking about this now during the real presentation?"

John: Yes.

Jim: So typically in your presentation package, how many pages are we talking about?

John: I'm looking at this one. It's 19 pages, and that includes some of the fluff. The first page is a picture of the building and some general information. I would say maybe four pages are boilerplate company stuff, how big we are and the way our team functions, the flow charts, the different focus that each of us has within the team. Really, the rest of it is all about the client and what we've determined to be their interest level, whether it be the data and valuation, or whether it be the process of how we're going to reach the target audience. It can vary.

Sometimes you get into more technical analysis. "How is the building valued and what can I do to enhance its value?" Sometimes we're focused in on the actual structure itself, talking about some of the things that would enhance value that are easy to do: a paint job, a parking lot job, a slurry and a recon. It can vary, but if you don't have that pre-meeting, or at least a pre-phone call, because sometimes that's all you can get and we acknowledge that, you're not going to know. It's important to have the pre-meeting, or pre-phone call with one of the decision makers, because otherwise a lot of times we'll get a call and you're meeting with ABC Company, and you don't have a relationship with them. Trying to get that pre-meeting, or the lack of getting one, can tell you a lot.

One of the things that we recognized a couple of years ago, and we've done it several times, is to say, "You know what? We're going to decline on presenting."

"What?! Decline?!"

Well, candidly, if we know that they have had a relationship or have been doing some business with a certain company, and a lot of times if you're worth your weight in salt, you will kind of know that...if you're the call with them that's a week before the presentation, they're just checking off the box because they need to hear three pitches from three different brokerage companies.

Jim: Absolutely.

John: If you feel as though you want to spend your time doing that, a lot of times we have no choice. We just have to take the shot. You just don't know. But sometimes you are that third presentation that they're going to just sit through because they are told by their boss that they need to sit through presentations from three different brokerage companies, but they've already selected who they want to work with.

Well, you can kind of figure out, either in the pre-meeting or by the fact that you're not getting one, that you're not a candidate.

Jim: I've got a story that I've got to tell you along these lines. Years ago, the team that I was working with was one of three teams from three different well-known brokerage companies that were going in to pitch on a listing opportunity. We're there in the company's office, waiting for our presentation time to come, and when the door opens, one of our competitor teams is walking out of the room. We go in and come out, and then when we leave, another brokerage team is waiting to come in.

So it was probably a 25-minute drive to get back to our office, and as we're driving back this light bulb goes off in my head, and I'm thinking, "Oh my gosh! I've got the perfect buyer for this building!"

Then I get back to the office and I call the buyer, and he says, "Yes, let's run down and take a look at the building." We go to the building, and he looks at it and goes, "I love it! Let's make an offer. I want to buy this thing."

So I call the lead guy on the decision-making committee for the owners and I say, "Listen, I've already got the buyer for this building. We can make the deal without even listing the property."

Then the response comes back to me: "No. I'm sorry. You're going to have to work through this other brokerage company, because we've already promised them the listing."

Then I said, "But you haven't signed the listing with them, have you?"

He responded with, "Well, it's already been promised to them, so you're going to have to work through them no matter what."

I just went, "You've got to be kidding me." We were just one of those three listing presentations that you talked about, where the box had to be checked off and they had to do their due diligence for corporate, but it had already been decided that the listing was going to go to this other brokerage company. Then we ended up cooperating with them and making the deal. My buyer bought the property and we closed, but our listing presentation was completely unnecessary, other than the fact that it at least put the light bulb in my head that I already had the buyer, and we made the deal.

John: Again, it's not an easy decision to make because there is that possibility that your assessment of the situation is not correct, but a lot of times you just know. I don't have any bashfulness in saying, "You know what? We're going to decline."

It happens maybe one out of ten times, and it is what it is. I think that your time is better spent actually cold-calling rather than preparing for the pitch.

I remember another thing that happened, or used to happen, because we now have something that we feel comfortable with and we can tailor it and modify it, and we know what we want to convey in a pitch. So before people would say to us, "We want you to come in and make a presentation." Then you'd just come out and yell to your group, "Stop what you're doing! We're putting together a pitch." It would take a week to get that thing from tee to green. That's a lot of time that's taken away from other activities that you could be doing that make you money.

Assessing whether or not you have a real opportunity, I believe, is one of those elements that you get out of that pre-meeting. Again, if you're getting the call a week before and you've never talked to them, there's a strong chance that you're not getting the business, because someone has already been talking to them. Unless they're completely incapable, the other company they've been talking to is probably the favorite horse.

Jim: Actually, along those lines, sometimes a good question to ask people in that pre-meeting or even ahead of the pre-meeting is the following one, "Listen, I just want to know that if we make a presentation and you like what you see and hear in our presentation, that you'll move forward, sign the listing agreement, and hire us as the brokerage team who will sell this building for you. Will this work for you?"

Then watch the body language and listen to the tonality in their voice, in terms of how confidently they agree, or in terms of how much they squirm and then hesitate. This can tell you a lot about whether or not there are other brokerage teams who are ahead of you in getting the listing.

John: That's a great point, and there are a lot of ways to ask that question roundabout. "Who's helped you with some of your real estate situations in the past? Tell me about that. Tell me more about that." Just keep prodding because a lot of times the last time you ask the question is when you'll actually get the answer.

Again, it's all about time management in our world of brokerage. There are a lot of different things we can be doing as a broker, and again, getting an assignment is of course what we all strive for. But if you've assessed the scenario properly and you can determine that you are a viable candidate for that, wonderful. If you've assessed that they've worked with CB on every deal, they called you with one week's notice on something that certainly has had to have been in discussion for a long time, and you're one of six, it may be a waste of time.

Jim: I tell people also, especially when you're dealing with the more entrepreneurial owners, the type of people who can sign the listing agreement at any moment in time and not have to go back to a committee...I think some-times it can be great if you do everything you can to schedule your listing presentation as the last presentation they're going to receive. Assuming that they're going to let everybody else make their pitch, they can't sign the listing agreement until they've heard all the pitches, and if yours is the last one and if you're at least in the running, or even a little bit better, you may walk out with a signed listing agreement, because they want to get moving and get the property on the market.

But in corporate situations it's a little bit different, because they can want to go back and talk about everything together, and then come back with the final decision sometime later on.

John: I think you asked it earlier, "If we're able to identify solutions to your problems in a manner that achieves your goals, are you prepared to hire us?" That's something that we will often throw up as a starter because we've had the pre-meeting. We'll say, "OK, we're here to address the issues that we've discussed. If we're able to achieve a satisfactory result with your understanding of how we're going to get you from A to B, are you pre-pared to hire us to move forward on executing the plan?"

Again, like you were saying, Jim, if you're getting a hem and a haw, then you know that you've got a little bit of work ahead of you. If you can get them all nodding, that should give you the confidence to go to the next step, which is to give them a presentation that addresses their needs, and then you'll have that level of confidence that definitely comes through. Your odds are pretty strong then that you're going to get it.

Jim: If you know you're dealing with an entrepreneurial person who has the authority to sign whenever they're ready, and they don't have to go to a com-mittee, and they don't have to worry about if they're looking good to some-body upstairs or anything like this, a question that you could ask them in the pre-meeting, or whenever it's appropriate, is you just say, "Listen, if we deliver a listing presentation that addresses exactly what you're looking for, and you feel confident that we are the team that you want to hire to work on this, are you in a position to sign the listing when we're done with the presentation?"

John: Engage us right now, yes.

Jim: Again, listen and watch the body language at that moment in time because a couple of things will be going on. If they're hemming and hawing, we just talked about what that could mean. If they say, "Yes, absolutely!", now you've sort of got them already committing that if you do a good job, that they'll sign the listing before you walk out the door, which is a great thing. Because otherwise now they've got to backpedal on what they said earlier unless they're willing to tell you what they didn't like about your presentation.

John: Exactly. You've set them up for, "If you didn't like me, you're going to have to tell me why."

A lot of times getting that verbal commitment, I've found historically, is about 75% of what you need. Many times people won't sign a legal document right there on the spot, but some entrepreneurs will. In my market we see it more often because we are mostly made up of entrepreneurs as opposed to Fortune 500 companies.

Asking for the business at the end of the presentation is something that we oftentimes forget, and it's important to do that because a) it's a trial balloon, or b) you're calling the question.

Jim: Yes.

John: A lot of times we'll pitch it. You'll sit down and they'll go, "Well that was very, very good."

You'll say, "So when is your decision-making process?" You should know all of that already, but a lot of times we will avoid the question we're afraid to hear the answer to. You've just got to ask it, because a lot of times you're going to get the answer you were looking for. If you don't, you'll have the ability to say, "Where is it that we didn't answer your questions?" Because if they're not willing to say "Yes", then you've missed something.

You just say it that way. "Obviously we missed on something that we wanted to share with you. Can you please elaborate on where we might have enhanced our presentation in terms of your knowledge? What area of our presentation didn't resonate?" Obviously, there are better ways to ask it, but you understand what I'm saying.

Jim: Yes. Obviously you've got your team, and how many people are we talking about? When you're going after listing opportunities, what are their responsibilities, and are they going into the room and making the presentation along with you?

John: It depends. We have a team of three salespeople including myself, and we have Kate who basically, as we like to say, "runs us". She keeps us honest with the commitments we make, and she's responsible for the marketing materials, both in the way of pitching, and around production. She executes all of the things that we do: mailing, creating the marketing materials, and basically everything.

What that then leaves is the group of three here: Patrick, who is someone who started with me about ten years ago who I trained, Jeff, who we brought on about six years ago who we also trained. Jeff is more of the cold-calling type. We're all different in our personalities. We're all different, and I think that is a very important thing in any kind of team, because if you have all three being the same types, you're not going to get the benefit of being able to resonate with different people. Jeff is a cold-caller. He loves the thrill of the kill. He's emotional about it. He's engaging. He's great at what he does...upturning stones and looking for opportunity.

We all do it, but he is driven to do it and really believes that this is his value added to our team. Patrick is more detail-oriented. He's what we call "the power". He's defined as being diligent, dependable, process-oriented, and detail-oriented. He will make sure that things are getting done. He's kind of quality control in a lot of ways in addition to cold-calling, and all those other things that we all do. He tends to follow through on making sure that whatever I generate in the way of a document is double-checked, and he will find the things that are wrong with it.

Then there's me. I started off as a cold-caller and as someone who wasn't part of a team. I started a long time ago with you, Jim. I tend to have a lot of those traits, but I'm definitely defined as what they call "influence" in this company, which means you're more of a "salesman" type. It's defined as enthusiastic, talkative, and engaging. I enjoy people, I enjoy hearing people's stories, I feel that I relate to people well, and I think that I bring that human part of things, the genuine part of things, because I believe I am genuine.

When I've asked people's opinion on this I've said, "What is it about me that works?" They've said, "You're just the real deal. You're not full of B.S." I think I *am* full of B.S. at times, but at the same time I think people consider me to be straight and honest, and I think that's another thing that I benefit from. I do place ethical behavior at a very, very high level in this business, because me getting away with screwing somebody over one time is going to come back to bite you. Most of the time when you try to screw somebody over, particularly another broker, a lot of times the deal won't happen, but you've still got the label on your forehead.

Jim: Yes, they will start talking to other people.

John: Oh, it's terrible. In this business you cannot afford to do that, because a lot of times your broker friends out there, or your competitors, are your biggest sources of information. If they trust you, there are a lot of ways to make transactions happen where you're able to get some secret sauce, some secret information, some information that might not have otherwise been given to you unless that person trusted you. That can be the difference between making the deal or not.

All of those elements come into play, but the way that we go into a meeting, if it's a big meeting, a lot of times all three of us will show up. We'll then be trying to assess who the other people are across from us. Hopefully we've had a pre-meeting and we've already been doing some guessing, but sometimes you get one person in the pre-meeting and he's got three people on his panel evaluating you.

A lot of times you're able to figure out who's going to resonate with who on the team. I think having that ability to go to the bullpen, if you will, and have me maybe take a step back and have Patrick lead the meeting, or have Jeff lead the meeting because he's resonating with the person who's across from him; those are the advantages you have by having different people at this pitch discussion, or even in just your initial discussions with a client, whether you're pitching him or not. You can kind of figure out who's connecting more with the person who's going to be the decision maker.

Having a diverse group really does help, but in the end, we're all salespeople. We all do the same tasks. Some of us are more gifted at other parts of it than others, but there's no substitute for all of us doing our prospecting, me more from the warm-calling with people who I've done business with, but you've got to stay in touch with them. I mean, it's a lot easier to keep a client that you've done business with, than to go out and find a new one.

Sometimes we lose track of the fact that five years have gone by and you haven't talked to this guy. You feel like you still know him, but he's already been talking to ten brokers in the interim, and he's forgotten you.

There's always something for us to be doing in the way of prospecting, but there are a lot of things that make up our business of brokerage, so many different little tasks, and it's nice to have a diverse group to accomplish those tasks, so we can match the right person to the exact task that needs to be performed.

Jim: We've got people listening who are solo brokers working on their own without a team of people around them. We've got people listening who are people who have teams assembled around them. I actually just want you to talk for a moment about how, if you don't have people around you to delegate to, you could easily be limiting your income in commercial real estate brokerage. I wanted to hear your thoughts on that.

I'm sure you started out way back when as a solo broker. You've gotten to the point where you've now got a team assembled around you, so you know the difference in how that all works. Talk about that aspect, and tell us when people may need to consider that it's now time to step up and have a team around them, instead of just constantly doing it all as a solo broker.

John: I think we have all heard management tell us, or have read books that talk about how the game has changed and how you can't do it solo anymore. I don't know if I fully agree with that, but I think there's a place for brokers who do things on their own, and I think there's a certain freedom that goes along with that. When you have a team, you're accountable to one another and that kind of keeps you all burning the same fire, if you will.

There are ways to do it where you don't have a formalized team. I set out to create one. I was very lucky that I was able to find people who I really like as individuals, who are my friends, who are very high-level performers in this industry. It was with a lot of thought and effort that I was trying to assess who I wanted, and that was difficult.

The other thing is that you have to make an investment. We talked a little bit about that earlier. The investment in time is probably one of the more costly ones, because in the end that's all we really have in our business is time. When you're taking time out of your day to make money and call and follow up and do all of the things we do to teach somebody the reins, that's a difficult scenario.

A lot of times you can achieve the goal of teaming by having a loose relationship with another individual in your office who you work well with, who you trust, who has a similar work ethic, who has a secret sauce that's maybe different than yours, a skill set that's a little different than yours, and you can come together on business that you might not get otherwise.

If you know your decision maker is the authority type, the accountant type, the one who likes rational, orderly decisions and back-up information; well, if you have a guy who has that kind of personality and you're the salesman type and he's not going to resonate with that, you're probably pretty well served to see if you can form some sort of loose relationship with this other broker in your office to go after business. Because 100% of nothing is still nothing, and 50% of some business that you would otherwise not get is, in my opinion, a nice bonus. So there are ways to achieve the goal of teaming without having that formalized structure, which some people don't like or can't do, especially older dogs in this industry which I, by the way, fit into that category now.

Again, I think that clients are much more demanding these days with the onset of email and instantaneous information by the internet, and being reachable anywhere at any time around the world via phone. Gone are the days when you can respond to somebody two days later via email. Your people are now expecting an immediate response.

I think that teaming is something that we will see continue. I think that it is a benefit to both the brokers who are a part of the team, but also to the clients themselves, but you cannot force it. That's the one thing that I'll leave everyone with. The concept of trying to force a team together because you just want it doesn't work. It's like putting gears together that don't match up.

There has to be some sort of natural flow and natural melding of this team, that there has to be some sort of commonality. I've seen a lot of teams form that break up. I'm sure we all have. For one reason or another they didn't work. Why? There are a lot of reasons why. One, they didn't have the same goal. Finding someone who you work with who has the same goal is hard. People are in different stages of their lives, and they have different motivations. Not everybody is going to have the same way of doing business that you do.

Being a team member, you need to be cognizant of that and understanding of that. Hopefully the work ethic works out the way that you all hope, and everybody's putting in their 50 cents to achieve the dollar, and it all works out.

You can't measure it deal to deal. On some transactions one person will be doing 75% of the work. Why? Because he resonated with the decision maker. Of course he's going to be doing 75% of the work. Hopefully there are other transactions where the scenario is reversed, to where he's not doing as much.

Again, it's hard to measure within a short period of time, deal by deal. I think even year by year it can be difficult, but if it works, you kind of know it's working. If it doesn't work, you kind of know that as well. There's no reason to force something that isn't natural, because in the end everybody's got to want the same things, otherwise the team falls apart quite quickly.

Jim: Very well said. We have a question from Stan.

Stan: Jim, thanks. Hey, this is my first round table conference call. First of all, John, thanks so much for sharing your time and your expertise. I've been in the business about the equivalent time as you, and you taught me some things and reminded me of some things as well. Thank you so much.

John: I appreciate that. Thanks, Stan.

Stan: A question regarding the pre-meeting: If you could tell me how you would handle this. Say, for instance, you're in a pre-meeting and it's determined by you knowing the market that the building's worth $100 a foot. The comps prove it, the current active buyers prove it, and this client that you're going to make a presentation to is insisting that they're not going to take anything less than $145 a foot. Again, this is hypothetical, but you and I have seen this before.

Would you decide during that pre-meeting, during that discovery period, that it's not worth pitching the listing, or would you kind of say, "Look, I'll try to pitch a listing if I can get them to accept reality. It's worth my time to put the team together and then make a full presentation."

In other words, have you ever pulled the plug in a pre-meeting not to pitch the actual listing?

John: Yes, I have, but I think a lot of times people will toy with people. There are a lot of folks out there who really want to understand your conviction. I've had a client do that and we got him into reality, but one of the things you need to do, in my opinion, is you need to ask a lot more questions.

For example, "Tell me, sir, what leads you to believe, based on the data that we've talked about, that your building is worth $145?"

He's going to then give you his opinion. Then you say, "Tell me more about that." Get him to keep talking. "If there was one last thing, sir, what would it be?"

A lot of times they'll say, "Well we bought the building for $130 a foot, and I'm getting a notice that it's in default."

All of a sudden now you've gotten a real confirmation to your suspicion that the guy is not able to deliver at market. Then you say, "I really appreciate your time, sir, but I don't know that we're going to be able to assist you, given that your situation is not one where we can achieve a value that's close to where you need to be."

Again, I think that just accepting what he says as, "I need $145", you're already thinking like this. Again, say things like, "Tell me more about that, sir. Tell me what leads you to believe…" Just get him talking. The more you just let him talk, you will get to an underlying reason. If he is presenting you with information, you say, "Look, I'm not a rocket scientist here. I'm just sharing with you the facts about the market. The building right across the street, the building next door, the building around the block have all traded in this range. What elements of your building lead you to believe that it's worth 45% more?"

If he can't give you an argument and you've exhausted all the questions like we talked about, then you've got a decision to make. But a lot of times you will find that the individual is just testing you. He's trying to figure out how much conviction you have about what you're telling him. Then you can also say, "Look, sir, can I be honest with you? Your building is 20,000 feet, it's worth $2 million, and you're telling me that you want to get $3 million for it. I can't do anything about that. Your building is very much related to the one that's in escrow across the street, and it's in escrow at x. The building right next door sold at this. Is there anything I'm missing here, sir? Because I don't know that I can help you."

He may say at that point, "Alright, I've now got this guy to believe what he's telling me, and I believe him now that he's gone to such lengths to explain it to me."

I don't know if that makes any sense for you, Stan, but I just think you always need to dig deeper to try to find out what the underlying reason is.

Jim: John, that's really good stuff, and another top broker who I've interviewed similarly just basically says, right along the lines of what you were just saying, just sit there with the comps right in front of them, the data with all of the printed information, and say, "Look, this building across the street sold for $100 a foot. It's very comparable to yours, so tell me, when looking at this data, what makes you believe your building is worth $150 a foot?"

When you ask them a question like that, they're going to have to run out of gas in their argument, other than digging in their heels and just saying, "Well, because I want $150 a foot."

Stan: Right, and like John said, at the end of the day you've got to make a business decision. Something with this much of a delta you're wasting your money on as an agent if he's going to hold to his $145. In terms of moving forward to an actual presentation, if he's still of that same opinion and you are selected, at that point maybe you tell him, "No."

John: Another thing is that you want to understand what's driving this. We talked a little bit about that, but let's say, for example, that there's an event. He's determined that he can't get a new loan, and that puts him in jeopardy of not being able to sell at market. Maybe the decision is to go ahead and say, "Look, we will try, because I understand that you think your office space would meet the needs of somebody, and it would cost a lot of money to duplicate that office space. So what we can do is perhaps try it at x price, which is 15% above market, but I need your commitment that if we exhaust that opportunity, that we will then deal with the reality."

He may say, "No, I won't", but you may also know information through your discussion and through your probing that he's got a loan coming due. Usually if you've got a loan coming due, the reality will take care of itself in many cases. Sometimes it's just, "Sorry, I can't help you." Again, I wouldn't leave it to just as you phrased the question. I wouldn't leave it to just, "No, I can't help you at $145", because he may be testing you like we talked about, or he may be looking for you to really prove yourself up to where he walks away from that meeting going, "OK, I believe this guy."

Stan: That's great! Your last comment, John, about getting the commitment: "If we exhaust all the $145 per square foot buyers, are you ready to get back into reality in say a 60-day period?" If he says "No", then obviously you want your competitors working on the listing, because they're wasting their time while you're out cold-calling and finding the real sellers.

John: Yes, listings are expensive from a lot of aspects, like time. You have to answer broker calls, you've got to show it, you've got to put together marketing materials, you've got to get the marketing materials out. There's a lot of stuff that needs to be done.

One thing that I will share is that we used to be about 60-65% on the agency side on listings, and then about 35-40% on the tenant-rep side. Well, we shifted that pretty significantly when the last downturn hit, because I recognized through experience that listings were expensive and the owners of properties in our market were more entrepreneurial, and they always were thinking that it was not going to be that bad, that it was going to get better.

They wouldn't react to the market and do what was necessary to move their properties. We decided we didn't want to be one of those teams having to deal with all the things you have to deal with as a listing broker with an overpriced assignment. We wanted to be on the tenant side.

A lot of times it takes a shift in your focus of who your clientele should be, because it's tempting to always take that listing. Maybe a sign call will move it, maybe a flyer offer, we all have those things on our mind. But in the end they are time consuming, and a lot of times an expensive endeavor where that time could be utilized uncovering tenants that you could be doing tenant rep work with instead.

Jim: And something else, too, is just make sure that you don't get wrapped up in beating your competitor for the listing so that you end up with a listing where you say, "Why the heck did I take this?"

John: Right. Winning is important, but not at all costs. The other thing is fees. In this market we're a little bit more stable today. Back in the last downturn, for a leasing assignment when there were 20 other alternative buildings, you needed to somehow separate yourself from the rest of them. Being different and saying, "Here's what I think will separate you from the rest. Here's a list of 20 buildings that you would look at if you were a user." You put them in the user perspective and you say, "Look, would you look at all 20? No. You're going to look at the ones that entice you. One is going to be the price. What could we do that would maybe entice people on price?"

The other is, "We've got to entice the brokers, and everyone else is offering three percent. I suggest we offer the brokers five percent or four percent. Let me show you how it will shorten up your time and you will achieve a higher value in a declining market." I can't tell you how many times we've done that in that kind of market and that separated us from the rest of the advice he was getting. We've been successful in winning assignments that way.

Jim: That's good.

Stan: That's terrific. Thanks so much.

Jim: Thanks for the question, Stan. We now have a question from Dawn.

Dawn: Hi. Thank you for this teleconference. It's been very informative. I was just wondering as a junior broker when you go in to pitch to get listings with your landlords, if there is some kind of script you recommend following. Also, if you're taking in a junior broker, what role do you recommend they play if you're walking in with a team of three?

John: Well, I'll give you a couple of perspectives. I think that as a senior broker, I've been involved in all sized transactions and still am to this day. One of the things that you could utilize, that I utilized when I was going up against a guy who had a lot more experience, was to get down to that genuine approach. You say, "Look, Mr. Landlord, I am not the person who has done all of the transactions on the street. I am not the one who has 20 years of experience, but what I have is a tremendous determination and a lot of shoe leather. I will cold-call the hell out of your project, or I will do everything I can to facilitate getting you the right tenant."

If you get them to understand that there are certain things that an older broker will or won't do... I mean let's be honest, I'm not going to be running around with 5,000 square-foot listing assignments. I have those projects, but I let others on my team handle those elements.

I think if you can differentiate yourself for the task at hand, I think that resonates with an owner. Yeah, the owner might think that the guy who did the $10 million lease down the street would be the right guy for a 5,000 square-foot leasing assignment, but if you can sit there and demonstrate to him that you really are the right person for that assignment, that's item number one.

The other one you asked is related to a pitch and a team of three going in. Well, when Jeff, my youngest partner, was on a pitch, his role, as I mentioned, and still is to a large degree, is the prospecting side. Well candidly, the value-add that a young broker brings to the table, I don't know if anyone can disagree, is their shoe leather, their phone abilities, and their time to spend cold-calling and dialing for dollars. That is the value to your team and to the client for giving you the listing. But if you're looking at it from a tenant-rep pitch, you're going to be the one who is generating the showings. You're the one who's going to be doing the analysis. You're going to be doing this and that.

Speaking to those facts and elements of the whole business I think is where your role is. I think, and I'll speak for myself, it would be silly for Jeff to be talking about all the transactions that the team has been involved in over the last 20 years, if he's only been in the business for six.

Again, I think that you just focus on where your strengths are within your team and sell those, because that's what the client wants to hear, especially sophisticated clients who have seen it all. They know that John DeGrinis isn't going to be cold-calling 5,000 square-foot tenants. But they know that Jeff will.

Again, I don't make any bones about it. "That is not my role to you, sir or ma'am. My role is to give you strategic advice once we have some scenarios that warrant opinions, and my experience is where my value comes in. Jeff would be the one cold-calling all these people. He will be digging up a whole lot of those alternatives. He will be touring the building, and I will know what's going on. But that's not my role." A lot of times as a senior broker that is what the client wants. He wants to see different tasks handled by different team members.

Jim: Very good, John.

John: Does that answer your question?

Dawn: Yes it does. Thank you very much.

Jim: Good answer, John, and delivered with such eloquence!

John: You're flattering me. My face is getting red.

Jim: I knew there was a reason I wanted to have you on one of these teleconferences all these years. We've just been like ships passing in the night with voicemail messages, and then I'd book someone else for the upcoming call. But I'm really glad that we did this.

John: I'm happy to help.

Jim: People might be running out of ink in their pens from writing down notes here tonight, and that's great. So in moving forward, John, I just want to say thanks so much for being on the call with us tonight. You did wonderfully. You did a spectacular job, and is there anything you want to say as we're wrapping up here?

John: Yes. It's not a sprint, it's a marathon. This business is tough, and one of the things that I've found is that there's a lot of rejection that goes on. There are a lot of books you can read that have influenced me, and *Think and Grow Rich* and *Who Moved My Cheese* are two of them, and they've really helped a lot of people who I have come in contact with.

One thing I will say is that when a door slams on your fingers and they get bloody from it, it's easy to want to just fold the tent, take the day off, and just quit. I just say, as it has been pointed out in some of these books, when a door slams on your finger, it means that another window just opened, and you've now got to find it.

When someone moves your cheese, there's always an opportunity there that we just don't realize. I think that's been some of the words that have guided me through some tough times in this business. With that being said, thank you very much for including me, Jim.

Jim: I greatly appreciate you doing this, John, and you were outstanding tonight.

INTERVIEW 4

Designing Your Brokerage Business to Maximize Success

Jim: Hi, this is Jim Gillespie, America's Premier Commercial Real Estate Coach^{sm} located on the web at www.CommercialRealEstateCoach.com. Tonight I am going to be interviewing our special guest, Scott Lamontagne, one of the top brokers in our industry. In addition we'll be taking some of your questions also.

With that being said, let me get into my introduction for Scott.

Scott Lamontagne is now the Managing Director of the Capital Markets Group at Jones Lang LaSalle, and prior to this he was a director with Marcus & Millichap's Institutional Property Advisors. Scott got into commercial real estate brokerage in 2003 and has achieved meteoric success since then. Within his first several years he amassed more than $370 million in closed multi-family transactions, and he became the number one multi-family broker in the entire state of Texas.

He was appointed Sales Manager of the Marcus & Millichap Dallas office in 2007, was appointed the Regional Manager for all of Los Angeles for the firm later on in 2007, and in 2008 he was appointed the Western US Director of Asset Services, becoming the firm's Senior Executive West of the Mississippi for representing lenders, financial institutions, and government agencies with troubled assets.

Today in his position as Managing Director of Jones Lang LaSalle's Capital Markets Group, he is responsible for their entire Central Texas region, and he's now closed and overseen more than $3.5 billion in commercial real estate transactions in the past 13 years.

In addition, year-to-date in the first six months of this year, Scott and his team have closed, listed, and have under contract over $600 million in multi-family investment and development site transactions, including the sale of a trophy high rise in downtown Austin, that has set the all-time price-per-unit record for the entire state of Texas.

With all of that being said, please join me in welcoming onto our call tonight Scott Lamontagne. Scott, thanks so much for being here.

Scott: Thanks for having me, Jim.

Jim: I appreciate you taking the time. I always search far and wide for people like you, guys who are just doing such a great job and are willing to take the time to teach other people about it, because there are a lot of people in our industry who produce some great results, but they don't want to talk about it and they don't want to take the time. So I greatly appreciate you taking the time to be here.

Scott: My pleasure.

Jim: I talked a little bit about your background in commercial real estate. I'd like you to tell us a little bit more about it, and also tell us about your background as a business owner before you ever got into commercial real estate, because I know in the coaching work that you and I have done together, especially when you were just a year or two into the business, that background in business, I felt, really had you understand how to market yourself as a business professional.

You've done so tremendously in commercial real estate. We're going to get into that, but so many commercial brokers don't do that great of a job of marketing themselves. I want you to talk about that business background and how it had you see what's necessary in marketing your own business, in any business, including commercial real estate.

Scott: Sure. When I started back in 2003, when you and I first met, I was six months in. That would have been roughly the beginning. I started half-way through 2003, and right at the end of 2003 is when we started working together.

When I first started, much like most of the Marcus & Millichap agents, you start on the private side and work your way up from there. I started with zero experience in real estate, but just having some desire and some interest in it. My background prior to that had been, as you mentioned, kind of a small business entrepreneur. I had many different businesses... smoothie franchises, technology consulting, and then if you remember, Jim, I had just sold a call center that I owned. I had taken about two years off and was interested in trying to purchase some real estate for my own portfolio, just some small, private stuff.

I kept coming across the commercial real estate offering memorandums and thought it would be something that I could sink my teeth into. Sales and finance were really everything that I ever knew.

I started in May of 2003. My first couple of transactions were just deals that I bought for my own account, just because I had a need to place some capital that I had from the sale of my company. In the process of that I kind of poked my head up and realized that you could really do well in this business. That's when I got serious and wrote a plan. I hired you, and we went to work.

I'll tell you that I think the biggest difference for me in how quickly we grew was really my perspective on building a business. When I came in, most everybody around me were one-off sales agents. They didn't have back office support. They didn't have marketing and business development systems other than the telephone. They didn't have websites. They didn't do any kind of advertising except for maybe some deal postcards. At best, the only other person that they might have on their team was one junior broker.

I looked at it differently. I really thought that this was a business that you could create a lot of leverage in, and certainly being the star quarterback of my own team so to speak, my focus was very quickly to replace myself in anything that was not revenue-producing very quickly. I don't want to give away too much of what we're going to talk about later tonight, but very quickly I wanted to hire that out and create a little leverage.

In the beginning, probably one of the most prominent things that I got from our time together, Jim, was the concept of really having a well-developed business development plan that exceeds just cold-calling. I think most brokers cold-call because they've got the time and they don't have the capital, or they don't want to spend the capital on investing in other areas of business development.

I think that's really the differentiator for me. I really came in looking to build a business versus just being an independent sales guy.

Jim: Sure, and that background is tremendous in giving you great insight to help you to do that. So many brokers get into commercial real estate not having been business owners. Maybe they were working for corporations or maybe they just came out of college or something like that. They come into an office, they look around, they see that all the other brokers in their office are only relying on prospecting, and oftentimes not getting their prospecting done.

When you see people who are veterans and they're not doing anything to market themselves and they're not mailing, it's easy to just say, "Great. I shouldn't be doing that either because if it was really successful and it produced results, other people would be doing it."

It's easy to get locked into this idea of, "Why should I do that because nobody else is?" But brokers are missing such a huge opportunity to differentiate themselves and position themselves in people's minds. I know we're going to talk about that a little bit later on, when we get into what you're doing in that arena.

In getting started, how important do you think it is for brokers to first have goals established that they know they want to be working towards accomplishing within their own brokerage businesses?

Scott: Jim, obviously that's paramount and it's a little bit of a lead-in question, but I'll tell you that's only half the battle. Goals are important, but goals without true accountability are just dreams. Part of what you have to do is you have to have real accountability. I think that's where there's a lot of breakdown. People don't really hold themselves accountable or don't have systems to hold themselves accountable to achieving their goals, and the incremental steps that it takes to achieve one big goal gets lost in the day-to-day grind.

Jim: Sure. So many times when it comes to goals, oftentimes the only time of year that the subject of goals comes up is at the beginning of the year when it's time to say, "What do I want to accomplish this year?" Oftentimes brokers may be working for managers who say, "I want to know what your income goals are for the year."

You mentioned the accountability, and that's extremely important along with this. This goes hand in hand with designing the game plan for what you're going to do to accomplish those goals, because just saying, "Hey, I want to make 50% more money than I made last year," but not writing down what you're going to do differently and how you've got to execute it week-to-week or month-to-month, is basically planning to fail. You're going to end up disappointing yourself, and it's extremely important to have both the game plan designed, along with the accountability.

For example, if you say you now want to make 20% more money than last year, the sum total of what you did as a broker last year is what had you make that exact amount of money. In order to make the next level, 20% higher, you've got to do some things differently, because just working it the same way is going to produce the exact same results, generally speaking, as long as the market doesn't really change much up or down. It's just extremely important to understand this concept and take a look at it.

Oftentimes, people don't look at their goals throughout the year. Oftentimes, managers don't ask brokers to talk about their goals the entire rest of the year until it's time to set the game plan again for the next year.

With that in mind, do you have any recommendations for brokers around this? Any recommendations for them in setting their goals or attacking them with the right game plan, or having that accountability that you talked about?

Scott: In the beginning, your goals and your game plan really are activity-based. If your goal is to close $1 million in gross fees, then you've got to start to break that down. Then your average transaction might be a $200,000.00 fee, which means that you have to close five deals at $200,000.00 gross in fees in order for you to achieve $1 million gross.

How many proposals does it take for you to get a listing? Well, you multiply that times five. How many appointments does it take for you to get that number of proposals? How many calls does it take for you to get the number of meetings that it takes for you to get the number of proposals, that you need to get the number of listings, that you need to be able to close the deals that you need? You just back into it.

In the beginning, it's very much activity-based. I would start with the end in mind and work backwards.

Again, that's only half of the situation. The other half of the situation is that you've got to have a carrot or a stick to help you achieve those individual pieces. I'm going to tell you, and we can all debate this, but in my experience, and certainly there have been books written about it, I'll tell you that the stick tends to work better than the carrot for most people. I would certainly categorize myself like that. I can tell you from a personal standpoint on our team, that we actually have a Board of Directors. When we set our goals we prioritize our goals. We do this quarterly and it varies, but we have very, very stiff penalties for missing our goals, very stiff financial penalties.

For somebody who's new in the business and maybe they haven't broken six figures yet, I've got one guy on my team who was brand new and his accountability was 100% community service oriented, no financial dollars. But the top brokers on our team might have a $1,500.00 penalty per quarter per goal for missing a particular goal.

When we come together, we have a Board of Directors. We have a couple of outside folks who are not on the team who sit on the Board of Directors, and they help us to manage all of our goals and accountability that we're doing, and they're making sure that we're not being too easy on ourselves from a goal standpoint. They're making sure that we're being hard enough on ourselves for missing goals. I can tell you that I try not to, but I have certainly paid some stiff penalties for missing my goals, too.

Jim: That is great! I've never heard of penalties that stiff before, but boy, that gets people motivated to make sure that they complete their goals! Having a Board of Directors for your team in brokerage, not a Board of Directors for the corporation you're working for, but a Board of Directors for your own team in brokerage, that's outstanding! That's awesome! I love that! It's just incredible. I tip my hat to you on that, as it's just phenomenal.

You mentioned the carrot or the stick, and I believe that that the stick works better with so many brokers. I think this applies in so many arenas in life, too, and sometimes the carrot on the stick is not nearly as effective as the blow torch under the rear end.

Scott: Well, there's no question. At the end of the day, especially because once you achieve success in this business money just becomes a way of keeping score, and once all of your needs have been met, it's difficult for the carrot to work.

When you're in the grind and you get busy, the last thing that happens when you get busy is the prospecting. When you get down to that point, the only thing that's going to force you to re-prioritize that is a big, fat penalty. And not only is it a big, fat penalty, but it's actually showing up with egg on your face in not having achieved your goal to your peers. I think those two elements are critical for brokers. Brokers first of all are ego-driven people by nature I would say. As a generalization, you would probably agree that that is a fair statement.

Jim: Yes.

Scott: We don't want to fail in the eyes of our peers, and we certainly don't want to give up anything out of our pocketbooks because we're all money-driven as well.

Jim: Yes. I think most people will fight much harder to keep somebody from taking $10.00 away from them, than they'll fight to make an extra $100.00.

Scott: That's a very valid point.

Jim: It's just that idea of somebody taking something away from you, you're going to fight tooth and nail to prevent that.

"As much as I'd like to make more money, if I don't make the extra call, that's OK because I've still got plenty of important things to do."

Speaking of making the extra call, how important is prospecting for brokers to develop more new business for themselves?

Scott: Obviously, again, Jim, it's another lead-in question. It's paramount. Clearly it's paramount. Most brokers will prospect pretty hard for the first couple of years in the business, and once they get their business going a little bit and they've got some pipeline and they're on to being busy with more things than just business development, they're executing and marketing on their assignments, they're executing the marketing plans, they're managing due diligence, they're negotiating contracts, and then once they get their first big wave of big commission checks, they're out buying boats and cars.

Then it's really easy for brokers to fall off of the prospecting bandwagon. In my experience, what I see is that the vast majority of brokers, after about two years in the business, really let their foot off the gas pedal on prospecting. Because of this, they never really get past it. They settle into this sort of comfort zone. Being comfortable in brokerage means making $250,000.00 to $500,000.00 a year. You can make good money and be comfortable and not work that hard once you get your business rolling.

There are a lot of people who never really progress past that point, and it's not because they don't know what to do. It's not a training issue. They fail because they fail to execute.

Jim: Part of that goes back to what you spoke about, about the comfort level after being in the business for several years. When you get started in brokerage, oftentimes you don't have very much money in reserve, so you're extremely motivated to do whatever it takes to get those first checks rolling in.

When you start making a decent amount of money, then all of a sudden the attitude can become, "I've got enough money in the bank for expenses for a number of months. If I don't make the calls, that's OK. I've got signs up, and somebody's going to call me."

It's easier, like you said, to take the foot off of the accelerator. So many times I find brokers just don't recognize how much it's costing them to not make those calls, because they're missing out on opportunities that they would have dug up had they been making the calls. I mean, they're going to find opportunities that otherwise would be going to their competitors. Opportunities to work on bigger transactions, and to work with people who might be more loyal than the people they're working with right now.

When you back off of making those calls, it's easier to hold onto all of the leads, including even the more marginal ones. When you prospect, you're digging up new transactions, better transactions, and you let go of the more marginal leads, because you don't have the time to work on them anymore.

Again, otherwise you're just leaving these leads to your competitors. You'll never even know that they existed, and that's why it's so important to keep prospecting to get those leads. Not only that, you upgrade the average size of your transaction and the average commission you're earning per transaction at the same time, because you're letting go of the more marginal leads, and you're finding newer and better and bigger transactions to replace those leads with. Life gets pretty good. You're making more money because the prospecting is developing newer and better deals, and newer and better opportunities with principals at the same time, too.

Scott: And I'll give you a way to quantify that. Part of what I think brokers ought to be focused on is thinking a little bit more like a CEO.

If you're a CEO of a company and you've got a sales rep, and that sales rep wants to make $1 million a year, and I'll use that number just because it's an easy, round number...the average person works 2,000 hours a year. That's $500 an hour if my math is correct.

My question is this: If I'm a CEO and I'm looking at a sales rep that should be generating sufficient revenue, that sales rep makes $500 an hour. If I look at that sales rep in the mirror, is that sales rep worth $500 an hour? Would I pay this guy $500 an hour to do what I do day-in and day-out on an hourly basis? If the answer is no, then you've got to change something.

Jim: That's an interesting analogy. It makes total sense, though.

Let's get into delegation. There are things that you want to do yourself and other things that you want to delegate. What are the activities that brokers really need to be doing themselves in their own businesses to be successful, and what activities do they really need to be delegating to someone else?

Scott: Perfect. It's very, very simple. Revenue-producing activity is the broker. Non-revenue-producing activity is not the broker.

Jim: So what would you consider as being revenue-producing activities?

Scott: Anything that could generate commissions. That's going to be cold-calling, client meetings, client events, which depends on what level of the game you're playing at, and any face-to-face client interaction. I do believe that marketing execution would be categorized as revenue-producing. In other words, if you've got a registration list and you're calling through that list of all of the people who are looking at the deal, and you're talking to them about the deal, that would certainly count.

Proposal review is revenue-producing, although anything that can be done by analysts or admin folks than can take the heavy lifting of the proposal work out of your hands is good, but certainly the final review process and things like that on proposals ought to be done by brokers.

Non-revenue-producing activity is executing the marketing plan. I'm not talking about the client call portion of that, but I'm talking about setting up the email blast, hiring the postcard vendor, getting the graphics package pulled together for the print shop, filling out paperwork for your firm to get the deal listed in your system, managing the escrow, pulling together the due diligence documents, writing critical date letters. Those are all non-revenue-producing activities, and those should be outsourced.

Jim: Absolutely. And what about things like preparation of proposals for listing presentations? What about those?

Scott: Again, the heavy lifting on that I want my back office to handle. I don't want a broker to take the time to be trying to assemble and crop pictures and all that kind of stuff. That's a back office function. That's a non-revenue-producing activity.

Let's go back to the $1 million a year analogy. Let me clarify this. So it's $1 million a year. The average person works 40 hours a week. I know some of you work a lot more and some of you probably work a lot less. There are 52 weeks in a year. With two weeks a year for vacation and holidays, that leaves 50 weeks. Forty hours times fifty weeks is 2,000 hours. Let's just say the average person works 2,000 hours, and if we're using $1 million, you'd divide $1 million by 2,000, and you'd get $500.00.

Your time at a $1 million net goal is worth $500.00 an hour, and here's the magic: If you can hire somebody to do it for less than $500.00 an hour, it should be outsourced.

Jim: Absolutely! I mean, let's face it. You can outsource activities, depending on what they are, for $15.00 to $50.00 an hour easily.

Scott: No question.

Jim: As someone who I've interviewed before, a great guy, an SIOR named William Hugron out of Orange County, California said, "If you don't have an assistant, you are an assistant." I've always liked that.

Should you be working on something that you could be handing off for $15.00 to 50.00 an hour when your time doing revenue-producing activities, prospecting, getting face-to-face meetings with clients and prospects, is worth $500.00 an hour, or even $200.00-$300.00 an hour?

You're much better off handing off that administrative stuff to somebody who can do it for $15.00-$50.00 an hour because that frees up time for you to make $200.00-$500.00 an hour by prospecting and having the face-to-face meetings with your people. It's a no-brainer when you look at it that way, but so many brokers just get so bogged down in feeling they've got to do everything all by themselves, that they can't see the forest for the trees around this. They can't see how much money it's costing them to not embrace this philosophy and this kind of behavior.

Scott: I'll submit to you that most brokers probably believe that it would be better to do it the way that we've been discussing, and that not letting go and micromanaging their business is really more of the problem.

The reality is that if you hire out non-revenue-producing activity, you've got to go do revenue-producing activity. And to do revenue-producing activity, you've got to do the stuff that you don't want to do.

Jim: Yes.

Scott: You don't want to pick up the phone and call, but you're forcing yourself to. Nobody wants to go do cardio, but we all know we've got to do cardio to be fit. It just has to be part of the business.

I think most brokers don't want to put themselves in a position where their sole responsibility is to do the things that they really don't want to do.

Jim: Yes, you'd be hard-pressed to find a broker who wakes up in the morning and says, "I can't wait to do more prospecting." But that prospecting is going to lead to great results.

Let's talk for a moment now about something that you've become very good at, and that's marketing. How important do you think marketing yourself to your clients and prospects is in terms of both becoming and remaining a top commercial broker?

Scott: Well, it's really important, but probably not for the reason that most people think. The reason it's really important is because there's an element of timing. I mentioned my call center earlier, and my call center happened to be a small business advertising consultant, for lack of a better word. We did all outbound calls, but one of the things that we used to do was we sold really low-level advertising. We sold refrigerator magnets with information on them and we sold advertising. We sold sports posters with advertising. They were just low-level, one-call-close type of stuff.

One of the ways that we used to sell refrigerator magnets was that we would simply teach the sales reps to ask the prospect what they have on their refrigerator.

OK, Jim, I'm going to ask you: Do you have magnets on your refrigerator? Yes or no?

Jim: Yes.

Scott: What's on your refrigerator? Give me the name of one magnet... one business.

Jim: Normally what we do is when we go on vacation to places, my wife will pick up a magnet that reminds us of the vacation spot. Actually, I can tell you one that we've got, and it's for an urgent care center nearby. Just in case we have an emergency, we know who to call.

Scott: Do you need that urgent care every day?

Jim: Absolutely not.

Scott: And when the need arises for the urgent care, where would you go to get the phone number?

Jim: To the refrigerator.

Scott: You'd go to the refrigerator, right?

Jim: Yes.

Scott: The point that I'm trying to make here is that timing is critical. In any purchase of any goods or services, timing is critical. It's not every day in my product group that somebody, especially on the private side, wants to buy or sell or refinance an apartment building. It's not every day.

If you're not marketing, you're gambling that the four times a year that you call that person is going to coincide exactly with when they have a need for your service. That's a big problem.

Jim: Absolutely.

Scott: If you're marketing, what you want to do is create top-of-mind awareness so that when the prospect is ready to make some type of a major decision with their real estate assets, that your name comes to mind. You've got to be one of the three guys or girls that they call to get the opinion of value, or to consult with them on what they should do. You have to be one of the three that they've seen enough times that they believe you've got enough credibility in the marketplace that they call you. You can't do that by cold-calling. The reason you can't is because you're only going to talk to them four times a year or six times a year, or, if you're really good, eight times a year.

You're sitting at a desk next to me and you're making 250 calls a week, and that's your business development plan. This is a real-life scenario. By my third year in the business, the guys who were the best guys when I started were still making 250 calls, or maybe even 150-200 calls a week. But they should have been making about 250 calls a week.

By that time, I had twelve agents on my team. By that time, I had a well-crafted email marketing campaign. I had a well-crafted postcard campaign. That guy sitting next to me making 250 calls, competing in the same marketplace as I was in, in the same product group, is now competing against me, and my team is making 3,000 calls a week. By the end of my third year in business, we sent out 250,000 pieces of mail.

Jim: I remember that.

Scott: Not including emails. All of a sudden, who do you think had top-of-mind awareness?

Jim: Absolutely. The clients had top-of-mind awareness of you and your team.

Scott: And it wasn't that we had 50,000 people in our database and we were mailing to them five times a year. We had 2,000-2,500 names in there and they were getting pieces from us constantly. They were getting emails from us constantly. They were getting deal cards and phone calls and everything else constantly. They were constantly seeing our name.

I would get calls, especially on the small private side, out of the blue saying, "I'm thinking about selling my property. Would you come talk to me?"

You just simply can't compete with that.

So how important is marketing? I don't know, Jim. You tell me.

Jim: It's huge! One of the greatest things in the world about it, with respect to commercial real estate brokerage, is that your competitors normally aren't mailing at all, or if they are it's very minimal. You put together a campaign like what you're doing, or even mailing just once a month. I ideally recommend mailing twice a month, 24 pieces a year, on top of your phone calls to people. As you've mentioned, you can only call them a certain number of times. Two times, four times, or six times a year at the max if they've got nothing going on. Because if you start doing more than that, they might file for a restraining order against you.

But 24 pieces a year of mail in their mailbox with information on what's going on in the market, and helpful tips...they'll appreciate the information, and you'll brand yourself within their minds.

I've heard so many times from my coaching clients the stories of their principals taking one mailer that they like and they stick it in the file for their property, then when it's time for them to do something, they'll go to the file, and there's your mailer and your phone number, and they just pick up the phone and call you. It's huge!

I've got brokers all the time telling me when I'm training them on how to do mailing for the first time, that within a matter of several months they're now getting phone calls from principals and they're excited. The principals are saying, "I like what you've been sending me in the mail. The wife and I are thinking of doing something with the property now, and we thought that you should be the broker that we call. Let's talk about this."

Scott: And Jim, think of this scenario. How many times have you heard this story? "I'm not selling. I'm not selling. I'm holding it forever. It's my retirement. It will be my children's retirement. I'm putting my kids through college with this asset."

The next thing you know, a lady calls you up and says, "My husband cheated on me. I'm getting rid of the property. I'm selling everything. Can you come talk to me?" Or, "Gosh, you know what? My wife is terminally ill. We want to go travel around the world. We don't want to deal with this stuff. Everything has changed. You know what? I hung up on you before, but I want to talk to you now."

One of the greatest things was when I managed an office in Los Angeles, I had a 20-year veteran who wasn't an institution-level broker. He was still a private broker, but just like clockwork he did really well. I asked him, a very simple broker, not a spectacular superstar broker by any stretch, but just a good solid role-player broker, "Would you come and do a workshop for the new agents in our office?"

I had him do a workshop, and one of the most memorable slides that I can ever remember from any training is that he put up a screen capture of his database notes on one contact. I kid you not, Jim. He probably had at least 25 entries over about a five or six-year period, and every single entry was, "Hung up on me, hung up on me, hung up on me."

Then all of a sudden, after 25 or 30 entries, all of a sudden it said, "Listed his property."

It's just one of those things. You have to be there at the right time and you've got to do the activities in order to get you in harm's way and get those opportunities.

Jim: Absolutely, and I remember one time several years ago, you and I were talking. You told me that you were managing or working with a broker who was relatively new in the business, and he was saying, "Why do I have to mail?"

You basically told him, "Look, I'm sending out over 250,000 pieces of mail a year, and you and I are trying to get business in the same territory. If you're not mailing, and I'm sending out over 250,000 pieces of mail a year, you're basically bringing a BB gun to a nuclear war."

Scott: Yup.

Jim: I thought that was a great analogy.

Scott: And listen. I'm not suggesting that people should be mailing 250,000 pieces or even 100,000 pieces of mail. It's expensive. I get that. But what you should be doing is touching them using various media types: telephone, email, not so much fax anymore because it's dated, but email campaigns and mail campaigns, and touching the client as many possible times per year as you can without them, like you said, filing a restraining order.

That still means email, and some people still respond well to email. People will generally look at a postcard. You get about a two-second view before it hits the waste can. That's all you need. It's an impression. You're trying to get a touch with them.

Jim, I don't know if you remember this, but when I first started, in my very first business plan that we put together I had a grid. It was a date-specific grid on when postcards, emails, and phone calls were going out. I started out, as I recall, with about 1,000 people in my database at that point in time. My goal that year was to have 40,000 touches. Every phone call, every piece of mail, and every email that went out was a touch. That was the goal. That's how we did it. I didn't have inventory then. I was just starting. I didn't have a lot of deals. I wasn't sending them four deal cards a month. It was, "Hey, if you're thinking about buying, selling, or refinancing, call me."

I don't know if you remember this, but we did two postcards...an A card and a B card...and we ordered them in bulk so it was cheap. I ordered 12 months' worth of the A card and 12 months' worth of the B card. Every two weeks we sent a little postcard out that didn't have anything to do with deals. All it said on it was, "If you're thinking about buying or selling, please call me." I had a couple of different versions of that.

The point was that I wasn't expecting to get calls from that, but I knew that if I did get calls from those 24 touches that I was going to get mindshare, and when I'd make the cold-call they were going to recognize my name. Because they had seen my name so much, I was going to have more street credibility and I'd likely get into a deeper conversation. It just became a self-fulfilling prophecy. As we began to list inventory then we added in the deal cards, and then we began to sprinkle those deal cards out as well.

In today's environment, we don't do nearly as much postcard mail as we used to. Obviously I'm doing much more institutional or major asset work in today's market, but we do have enough inventory volume and we're doing enough deal marketing that our name is seen two, three, four, or five times a week anyway. You build into that, but in the beginning, you've got to create ways and reasons to touch your clients and prospects.

Jim: I remember when you were just getting started in the business and you said, and I'm just paraphrasing here, "Through this marketing campaign that we're going to be embarking on here together, after about two to three years in the business I want to have created the impression in the minds of the people that I want to do business with, that I've already been in the business for ten years, and that I'm a seasoned veteran."

I just thought that was a great way of looking at it, and you really achieved that in such a short period of time.

Scott: Actually, I believe it was a 20-year brand in a one-year period. That was the goal when we started working together.

Jim: Alright. Well, that definitely sounds like the Scott Lamontagne of today!

Scott: That was what we were trying to accomplish. I don't know if we necessarily accomplished *that*, but I think that sometimes when you shoot for the stars and you miss it by a little bit and catch the moon, it's not a bad thing.

I'll say, just for the record, that starting with zero experience with no senior mentor to work with, I went from zero to by the end of year three, I closed 56 apartment transactions, I had 12 agents on the team, and by that point in time we were easily the number one team in the southwestern region of the country for our entire firm.

Jim: That's incredible! You mentioned that you're sending out over 250,000 pieces of mail. Just out of curiosity, you're sending that out to how many principals in total now?

Scott: Part of that was that we used to be able to buy into a postcard for the entire office. All the agents contributed their databases to a third-party situation. Then you could put your deal on the postcard for $250.00 for a small picture, and it had your name and phone number or email address under your deal. Or you could do a half page. It was an 8 ½" folding larger postcard and there were two big deals on the front that you could buy for like $400.00 or $500.00.

I think that one went out to 10,000 people at a time. So part of my 250,000 was this pooled scenario. The other portion of that, probably about half of it was to our database. By that point in time, I think we were probably working with 3,500 names with good addresses in our database, or something like that.

Jim: Got it.

Scott: But every deal got a listed postcard and a sold postcard. This was after inventory began happening. Before that they were just generic postcards that had different messages about seeing my name and my brand, and a "Call me if you need me" kind of a statement. Basically, they were generic marketing and branding pieces.

Then as we had deal flow we would do a postcard for the listed, a postcard for the sold, and then twice a month we were doing inventory postcards for the team. If we had 12 deals listed, then we did a postcard and put the 12 deals on it. Then on the back of the card we would put all the deals that we had under contract, or just recently closed.

We would purposely leave bits of information off of those comps so that they would call us to talk to us about the comps, etcetera. That was basically our mail campaign.

Then we did research reports and things like that as well. In addition to that we did a weekly email blast. Tuesdays at 1:00 p.m., and we would do this religiously. We would do an email blast that would go out with all of the available inventory with links to the most recent research reports, etcetera. Very specifically, I tied in something else. When we did that first marketing schedule, we had dates, and again, accountability.

We had dates in there when all of these postcards had to drop...all of the non-deal cards and the research reports on a quarterly basis. They all had to be mailed out on a specific date. Whatever that date was, at 5:00 p.m. on that day that card had to be out. My staff had their bonuses set on one trigger. They were eligible for bonuses on a deal-by-deal basis, but they did not get paid their bonuses that month if they missed that date.

Ask me how many times the staff didn't get paid a bonus.

Jim: How many times did the staff not get paid a bonus?

Scott: Zero.

Jim: There you go.

Scott: They got paid a bonus every single time they were due one. The reason is because I made that a priority as the leader, and they knew this was a priority, and I tied their compensation to it.

Jim: That's great! I mean again, the huge incentive, or the "I don't want to lose this money if I don't get this done" kind of an attitude. That's great!

Again, if the stick works better, or the blow torch under the rear end works better, that is real incentive because they know you mean business, and they're going to get it done for you. I love it!

Scott: The last thing in the world you want to do as a manager is to force yourself into a situation where you're going to have to micromanage the team. I very clearly had just a few major, very important items, and their compensation was directly tied to it. That way I didn't have to say, "Hey, gosh, Jim, did you get your postcard out at 5:00 p.m.?"

They made sure I knew that it was out!

Jim: Not only did they get it done, but they made sure that you knew they had gotten it done. That's great!

Scott: Honestly I've got enough ADHD in me that I don't have the capacity for the detail. Unless it's in my Outlook calendar with a task, I literally would not be able to remember to follow up on it. You want to build your systems and processes to where that accountability is built in, but that's a different conversation.

Jim: You mentioned the growing size of your team over the years. How many people are on your team now, and how do you go about delegating different responsibilities to everybody on the team?

Scott: Last week and this week are different. As you know, Jim, I'm in transition. I spent the last three years on an Institutional Property Advisors Texas team. There were three principal brokers, myself and two others. At the peak we had a total of 18 people, but generally we kept it to about a 15-person team.

There were three principal brokers, and three or four junior brokers on the team, and then all of the rest were back office support staff, and they all had different functions. We had research, admin, analytics, graphic design, marketing, and then some of those positions had multiple people, depending on our volume and things like that.

Jim: So that's a pretty substantial-sized team right there.

Scott: Yes, so now I'm making my transition to JLL, and part of what we'll be doing is having to hire and build up the back office for the existing team. There are going to be three brokers starting out. Central Texas has two primary markets in it, which are San Antonio and Austin. I'll have a lead broker for the San Antonio MSA market. Then I have a broker on my team who will be managing Austin as the lead broker there. Then we'll hire a secondary markets broker or team to focus on the secondary and tertiary markets...the Corpus Christi's of the world. Then we'll have a land team.

The first thing you can do in the spectrum of the asset cycle for multifamily is acquire land to do new development. We need to be able to be turnkey and we want to have every facet covered. So we'll have a land person, secondary markets, we'll have Austin and San Antonio, myself as a lead, we'll have a debt structure guy, we'll have an equity sourcing individual, and then we'll have a full back office. The back office, again, will be administration, research analysts, financial analysts, marketing, and graphic design.

Jim, I'm going to add one more thing in there because I want to prove to you that I buy into what I'm talking about around outsourcing anything that's less expensive than the value of my time. I have a driver that I use a lot. Because I go back and forth between San Antonio and Austin, and frankly it's about as fast to drive to Houston and Dallas, and that is where a lot of the clients are that own in the Central Texas marketplace. I spend a lot of time in a car, about 3,000 miles a month, so I use a driver quite a bit.

It's not full-time yet, but at some point in the very near future, part of my team will include a full-time driver. I've even contemplated some mobile office capabilities, too. But for the time being, I do use a driver part-time so that I can be focused on having an office in the car.

I hotspot off of my phone. I've got my laptop and my headset and my cell phone. I'm making deal calls or prospecting calls the entire time I'm driving.

Jim: When you first said, "I use a driver quite a bit," I thought we had segued into talking about your golf game suddenly.

Scott: Trust me, you would not be interviewing me on that!

Jim: The British Open is just about to start and they're talking about how the course this year will have guys teeing off with two-irons instead of with woods. So I thought, "OK, this is a natural segue." Then I realized you were talking about your car. But again, it's about maximizing your productivity.

If you can be productive during that drive time and pay somebody less than the $500.00 an hour, or whatever your rate currently is, that's a productive use of your time to hire somebody to do that for you while you're on the road. Again, I greatly admire you walking your talk and recognizing that, and then hiring somebody to do that for you.

A lot of the people listening are going to be brokers working within an office on their own, and they won't be on a team. Maybe they've got a partner, and there will be managers or owners of brokerage companies listening, too. With this in mind, when does a broker need to hire somebody to delegate to in their brokerage business?

Scott: That's a great question! I worked with a lot of brokers when I was a manager on this topic, and I'm going to tell you that the first key indicator, the first sign that you're not creating leverage in your business, is that you've dropped out doing your prospecting.

Jim: Very good!

Scott: Your prospecting has now become last. When that happens, you're not bleeding money, you're losing money. You're losing opportunity cost.

Keep in mind that if your goal is to make $1 million a year, and that's $500.00 an hour, and you're licking stamps and stuffing flyers into an envelope, you're paying yourself $500.00 an hour to do a menial task. Not all tasks in the back office are menial. I'm not suggesting that, but I am suggesting that you can outsource every non-revenue-producing activity in real estate for far less than my price point. As you mentioned, $10.00-$25.00 an hour, or $10.00-$30.00 an hour is typical.

From a timing standpoint, that's how you recognize when you need it. Then from a timing standpoint, when is the right time? I believe that when you're a new broker, it's when you have six months worth of personal expenses and business expenses saved up. When you've got six months worth of business and personal expenses in your checking account, and you have good deals in the pipeline. You can't have just closed a big deal and now you've got the money, but you've got no other listings, and you've got no real prospects. You've got to have pipeline.

In other words, you've got to be to the point where you can see some sustainability to your income. As soon as you hit that point, you need to hire an assistant.

There are some things that will naturally pull brokers away from shoring-up their back office: 1) Brokers are eager to have junior brokers, because they think having junior brokers creates more revenue. 2) Brokers tend to want to buy deals. We're in real estate because we believe in real estate. We love real estate; it's a great game. We love the adrenaline of it, but every broker I know still wants to own deals. They get focused on trying to buy their first deals. They're in a hurry to get their first deals. 3) As brokers we get paid in big buckets. We get a big bucket of money and we want to go buy a Mercedes. We don't want to do the things that we know we need to do to grow our business.

The reality is, if you're a good broker, your own time is the best asset that you have. If you go hire a junior broker, you're going to get paid 50% to go support them build their business. That's a hard concept for a lot of people to get, but the reality is, a junior broker is going to set appointments. You're going to go on their appointments, and it's going to take your time, and it becomes dilutive to your business if you're not prepared for it.

If you trust yourself and you're right for the business and you're truly a good broker, then you need to seek to maximize your revenue-producing time above and beyond all else. By hiring an assistant, and by an assistant I don't mean a $10 an hour task manager who's going to be sitting there waiting for you to task them. I'm talking about somebody who can run your back office. So maybe "assistant" is not a good term for that.

Once you get busy and once you get your first five or six listings and you're processing them and you're executing them and you're marketing and you're managing the escrows and you're trying to get the deals closed, the last thing on your mind is doing more prospecting because you're busy. But what if somebody else was managing all of that for you, and now you could just be focused on bringing more revenue in the front door?

You're going to pay that person. Jim, you tell me, you work with a lot of people across the country. What's the average for a good, college-educated executive assistant or personal assistant, or a project manager? Call them what you want...somebody who can actually manage your back office. What would that cost you?

Jim: Are we talking about somebody full-time working in your office?

Scott: Full-time. What do you think that might cost on average? $45,000.00 or $55,000.00?

Jim: It just depends on where, and who the person is. Yes, I would say, normally speaking, depending on who the person is, $45,000.00-$65,000.00. But I've seen some guys who I've worked with who recognize how important it is to make sure this person stays with them, and has no incentive to leave. They make sure they're paying them really well. Sometimes they give them spiffs and percentages of everything they close. Sometimes these people can end up making over six figures. If they're looking at going someplace else and thinking, "The best I can do someplace else is making $65,000.00," they're not going to go anywhere. With this in mind, you simply don't want to have to train a new person from scratch all over again.

Scott: So let's talk about that. Let's say you get a great person for $100,000.00 a year, and I'm willing to bet you that you could hire a great person for that money. As a matter of fact, this person is no longer an administrative assistant. They're no longer a project manager. For $100,000.00 a year, you've just hired yourself a COO.

Jim: Understood.

Scott: Let's say your average fee per transaction as a broker is $200,000.00. I don't have experience on the leasing side, so I don't really know the metrics there.

Jim: You're earning a much higher amount per transaction than most brokers. I would say if you're talking about the average broker in the business, their average commission is going to be somewhere between $10,000.00-$30,000.00 per transaction, including leasing commissions, too.

Scott: Gross fee?

Jim: Yes.

Scott: OK.

Jim: I'm talking about all brokers on the average, including all sales and leasing commissions.

Scott: So let's do the math. Let's just say $100,000 per transaction for easy math. Is that fair?

Jim: Yes. We can always adjust the math.

Scott: A million dollars at six percent is $60,000.00. A two million-dollar deal at five percent is $100,000.00. I think probably everyone on this call is capable of doing a $2 million deal. I'm going to put it to you this way. When you get busy, Jim, what do you think, maybe 70% of your time is spent on doing non-revenue-producing activity?

Jim: Yes, that can happen very easily.

Scott: You're out doing inspections and you're trying to gather due diligence documents. You're finding excuses to do marketing plans, and you're not prospecting. I think the 70% may actually be a conservative estimate.

You hire this $100,000.00 a year person. You're probably going to do six-to-eight deals, maybe ten deals a year on your own with no help, and you're going to be busy. When you hire this person, you're going to get 75% of your time back. Let's say that because of training and some oversight, you're not going to get 75%, but more like 50% of your time back. So for $100,000.00 a year, you're going to get 50% of your time back. If instead you're closing deals at $50,000.00 or $60,000.00 fees, then you're probably not hiring a $100,000.00 a year person. Maybe it's a $45,000.00 a year person.

Jim: Absolutely, yes.

Scott: My point is that one or two more deals a year pays for that person. You're crazy not to hire that person first and get all of your time back. You're crazy! If you did nothing else but hire this person to run your back office and you backed off and stopped working 50 hours a week, and started working 30 hours a week, you'd still make more money and be happier.

Jim: Yes.

Scott: So why would you not do that first? The reality is that most brokers are focused on trying to get juniors, because they're trying to add fire power to the team. I'm going to tell you that if you'll build good systems and processes and put good people in place, that you could add a lot of fire power and have it not be dilutive to your business. I'm going to give you another example...

In 2006, my third year in the business, I told you we closed 56 deals. We had 12 agents on the team at the time. We had two back-office people. Honest to God, we had two full-time back-office people and we had plenty of capacity. A lot of that is because we had such a focus on building management systems into our back office, technology management systems. So the staff of two could execute on a lot of stuff for us.

I wasn't doing institutional transactions back then. Those are more time consuming. I was doing private transactions, but we had 56 closed deals. I don't know what the real statistics are, but we probably had 70 listings to get 56 closed deals in a year with two full-time back office people.

We did have part-time interns during the summer, but generally those were people trying to add more to our database. So they really weren't back-office people.

Those are my thoughts and my opinions. It's the need, and the whys and the hows and the whens. By the way, I have never seen a real estate deal that could pay you a return high enough such that you should do that deal instead of hiring your assistant who gives you 50-75% of your time back.

Jim: That's very important information. So many brokers need to hear this and need to understand this, because so many brokers can get completely bogged down. Their attitude can oftentimes be, "But wait a second. That's money that's going to be coming out of my own pocket. What happens if I don't bring in the new deals now at the higher level?" They stay at the lower level because they're afraid of making that jump, and in many ways doubting themselves being able to come through at the new level. As we've said, once you've got that stick hitting you, or the blow torch, you rise up to a new level, and you make sure that you make it happen. But you've got to be willing to take that leap of faith and go for it.

Scott: If you don't believe that with 50% more time you can get two more deals a year, you don't need to be in this business.

Jim: In addition, let me just mention this. For people who are doing only sale transactions, the commissions per transaction will most likely be higher. When you've got an office building for lease, and you've got to lease out 500 square feet to somebody, and it's a three-year lease, that's going to knock your average fee per transaction down. These brokers are doing a higher number of transactions with lower average commissions per transaction. So you're in a different arena when compared to what brokers are doing in sales. So when you're a leasing broker, you might do 30-70 transactions per year.

Scott: Sure.

Jim: So the next question around this is, talk for a moment about how if you didn't have anybody to delegate all these activities to, and you were trying to do it all by yourself like so many brokers are still trying to do today, what would your life be like, and what would your commission revenue be like?

Scott: Jim, it's just this simple. I would not be on this call tonight. You would not be interviewing me. I'd be a no-name, me-too broker who's just out getting a couple of deals done a year, probably making an OK lifestyle. I just don't know how to explain it any better than that.

I'd be miserable because I'd be having to manage the entire business, and I don't believe that I'm really all that great of a manager. I'm certainly not capable of managing detail very well. It would be a miserable spot for me for sure.

Jim: So when it comes to hiring that assistant, let's say a full-time assistant, but it could be a part-time assistant for some people, do you have any recommendations on how to recognize that you're hiring the right person for the job?

Scott: I really think that you have to be thinking in terms of you being a business owner, and you're really hiring somebody to run half of your business. The way that I thought about it, and again on these calls that we've done together over time, Jim, I've always gone back to the beginning when I was doing private deals at Marcus & Millichap, because that's probably more relatable for most people.

My first assistant I fired in four months because I made a mistake. I hired an assistant. This was a low-level administrative person. I can't remember if she even had a college degree, but she wasn't capable of doing what I needed her to do, which was to actually own my back office. She needed to be able to completely own and control my back office. As a matter of fact, she needed to be able to chase me out of the back office, and she was really waiting for me to tell her what to do next.

I'm going to suggest to you that that way that I looked at it was I was the CEO, but I only had 15 minutes a day to be CEO, because my more important role and where I needed to spend 85% of my time was in being Vice President of Sales. I needed to have a VP of Operations, or a COO, or call it what you want. That person had to be my peer, because my primary responsibility was to be the chief sales guy. That person is going to be the head of the back office and we're peers. Even though I'm the CEO, I only want to wear that hat for 15 minutes a day. That person had to be capable of completely owning that space.

We had quarterly meetings. You can't do everything at once, so we set goals and priorities. The team would put in recommendations on how we wanted to beef up our systems and our processes, and all that stuff. We would do a timeline over the next quarter, and we'd break it into pieces. We'd have some accountability and all that, but the reality is none of that worked without having a chief running it. In this case, my guy's name was Carl. Carl was capable of running it, and he was very detail-oriented. He was very systematic and process-oriented. As brokers and as salespeople, we have a tendency to be less granular than somebody who should be in this role.

I'm going to suggest to you that you want to hire somebody who is going to manage or be fully responsible for the entire back office. When I hired Carl, I literally took him from the reception room. I shook his hand. I welcomed him, and I brought him in and showed him where my filing cabinets were. I said, "These are my filing cabinets. If I ever know what's in those drawers, you're fired."

That is a true story. I really did that. My point wasn't that I wanted to be a jerk, or mean, or difficult, but I wanted him to know that this was his territory. This was his turf, and even if I needed something, every broker on my team was instructed that anything you need in the back office goes through Carl, and then he would assign that to his staff. We built such great systems and processes, everything went through Carl, and then Carl was the air traffic controller for the entire back office.

He was responsible for critical dates and timelines. He was responsible for executing the marketing timeline and getting the blasts out on time, and again, his bonuses were tied specifically to not missing those dates.

He would chase the brokers down. If they needed investment drivers for a book, or he needed to get bullet points for a postcard and the broker was missing their timeline, and his timeline was about to be up, he would start out a couple of days early and put it in their calendar. He would be responsible for being the person who would actually set the task up in the calendar. If they missed their timeline he would notify them. Or if a buyer, for example, didn't sign a Receipt of Documents letter or something, and he was about to miss his timeline, then he would escalate it to me only if, after he had followed up twice he couldn't get it accomplished. At that point in time he would come to me. I'd put my CEO hat back on, and I'd go make it happen. Short of that, he was responsible for 100% of my back office...period.

When you go to hire the person, you go to hire somebody who is going to be capable of running part or all of your back office.

Jim: That's great advice. You mentioned the mailing that you do. Do you do anything else to stay in relationship with your past clients to help ensure that you're working with them again on their next transaction?

Scott: One differential from the institutional or major asset world to the small, private world is that the higher up the food chain you go, the more that the meetings become focused on economy and market information. They're looking for you to be the street-level or reconnaissance-type provider of information. It's very different. With the private client, it's much more of an asset-specific role, trying to talk to them about making moves in their portfolio that are going to help them achieve a greater position.

It is a little different, but we do a lot of research-driven, very granular submarket driven construction pipeline data and comps, and rent structure and trends and economic trends and macroeconomic trends. We come into business development meetings. We do, generally speaking, a couple of different lists. I'm not going to give you all of the trade secrets, but we have our clients broken down into a few different lists. I can tell you that if they're on one of those lists then we tend to do a road show in the fall and the spring. We make sure that we go and sit in their offices. It doesn't matter what city they're in. We go and we get in their office, whether it's Austin or San Antonio, or Dallas or Houston, Chicago, New York, or L.A., or you name it. We're going to be on the road to go sit in front of them and we're going to have these market updates. That's one area where we do that.

Another thing that I do, and I would certainly recommend this, Jim…you know as well as I do that you're an expert if you're standing in front of them in the room. I try to do as much speaking as possible, and I speak at a lot of the trade shows and at a lot of the multi-family events. I speak at virtually all of them in Texas, generally, every other year. That's another area.

Then of course, we're in a fortunate position now where we've enjoyed a full pipeline for many years. Part of that means that you're getting your name out in front of clients because your name is on deal cards, and you've got "Just Listed" and "Just Sold" cards going out, and you've got four or five email blasts in the marketing campaign going out for each deal, so they're seeing you constantly.

For me and for our execution, almost everything is done on a bid basis versus a first-in, first-out basis, so there's a call date for the bids. We're working the process up to the call date. I'm having interactions with the acquisition teams and the officers. Sometimes it's the principals of the company and sometimes it's the equity people, but most of the time it's the acquisition people. I'm getting a lot of touches in, just in my day-to-day activity as well.

Jim: Sure. If there's a broker out there who is basically working on their own within an office and they're thinking, "OK, should I hire an assistant to work for me, or should I consider forming a team with other brokers in the office, so we can delegate and share responsibilities among ourselves together?", what advice would you give them to help them to make sure they're making the right decision?

Scott: I think you need to look in the mirror and you have to make some realistic judgments about yourself, about what you're good at and what you're not good at, and what you're willing to do.

The other magic to all of this, Jim, and the reason why you mentioned that I'm willing to share this information with everyone, is because I'm pretty much an open book. I'll tell you everything I do, and guess what? 99.99% of the brokers out there just aren't going to execute on it.

Jim: That's just the way it is.

Scott: It's just a simple fact. Do you want my database? It's public knowledge. You can have my database. If you're not willing to go out and create the relationships, it's just not going to matter.

You've got to be realistic with yourself. If you get all your time back, would you really do more prospecting? If the answer is "yes" then you could, hypothetically.

When I was in Dallas and we had our mid-market team that I've been talking about most of the night tonight, there were a couple of agents who would generally outsource most of their deals to us. They would get the lead, I'd help them land the client, and then my team and my back office would run the whole deal, and we'd split the deal with them 50/50.

It took a couple of touch points with my time. It took a little bit of time on their side, and everybody made more money, so everyone was happy.

Those guys leveraged us. They basically outsourced their entire process to us, and they looked at themselves as just being lead generators, which is an interesting concept.

Jim: Yes it is.

Scott: In terms of building a team they said, "My strength is that I'm good at just turning up leads, and I want to be able to go home at 5:00 p.m. and see my baby. I don't want to have to work that hard, so I'm going to outsource the entire process. By the way, I'm going to increase my odds now, because I'm going to have this market leader on my appointments with me landing the deal, and his whole team is going to execute everything, and I'm going to collect a paycheck at the end." That worked. There was one individual that did it very frequently, and I've had many others who have done it from time-to-time.

That individual took note of his own skill set and what he was willing to do, and he said, "I can make more money and I can increase my odds, and I can do less prospecting by just being a lead generator." That was one way to look at it.

I think again, it really comes down to really just knowing yourself and what you're willing to do, and knowing what you're really capable of.

Jim: When you said that you could tell everything about your operation to the entire brokerage community and very few people would do it, I completely understand that. The number one reason why people will hire me for one-on-one coaching is the same as the number one reason why they don't, and that's accountability. Oftentimes the people who come on board with me say, "I'm ready. I'm sick and tired of not getting this stuff done and I know that if I work with you you're going to hold me accountable and I'm going to get it done." Then there are other brokers saying, "Oh, this sounds like a really good idea, but I'm just kind of comfortable doing what I'm doing and not getting it all done, and being held accountable seems like it would be a big jump for me."

I've had musician friends over the years. They told me about an old joke in the music industry that goes, "How many lead guitarists does it take to change a light bulb?" The answer is five. One to do it, and four to just stand there and say, "Hey, I could do that."

Scott: Right.

Jim: It's often very similar in brokerage.

Scott: I said it earlier and I'll say it again. People in this business normally don't fail because they don't know what to do; they fail because they don't execute.

Jim: Absolutely. Tony Robbins had a great quote that I heard him say years ago. He said something very similar to, "A great coach is someone who teaches you to do what you already know how to do." So many ideas that we talk about in these teleconferences, some of them are new to the people listening, and maybe they've never heard them before, especially the people who have recently joined the program. But some of the ideas you're hearing for the second, fourth, fifth, eighth, or tenth time. Hopefully there comes a moment in time where you say, "I'm sick of hearing these ideas and not implementing them, so now I'm going to do what it takes to implement them."

Then there are some people who will say, "You know, I'm sick of hearing all these ideas and not implementing them, so what I'm going to do now is not be in the program anymore, because if I don't hear these ideas anymore, at least it's not bothering me that I'm not implementing them."

It just depends on where you're playing the game. Something that I'm curious about...when you get a listing on a property, how frequently are you following up with your owner and keeping them informed on what's going on, and how do you get this done--verbally or in writing? I imagine someone on your team will be responsible for this.

Scott: Yes. It's weekly. My marketing manager is responsible for all that. It's a draft. The lead broker provides some input to that draft, but that marketing manager is responsible for it. I don't let the brokers have responsibilities for non-revenue-producing activity.

Jim: And you do it weekly, because that's always a big complaint with owners; that they never hear from the broker. When the broker has no activity going on, sometimes they can feel like they just want to disappear and hide because they're embarrassed about it, because when they delivered the listing presentation they talked about what a great job they'd be doing at marketing the property, and how they'd be producing a ton of activity. But when there's nothing going on, the broker can feel like they just want to hide, and that makes the owner feel like you're not doing anything.

As you get closer to the listing expiration date, then they're going to say, "Since they're not doing anything at all, why don't I just hire another broker instead of extending the listing with them?"

So communicating with the owner every week is outstanding.

Scott: Again, it's a different conversation, but if you're doing price-listed deals and not doing a bid-basis scenario, let's say you've got a $2.5 million listing and you've got no offers at the end of the marketing period. The owner is naturally going to blame you first. They're going to say, "Gosh, that broker made me all these promises and he didn't execute on them. As a matter of fact, I didn't even hear from him. He's just sitting there with his feet on his desk waiting for the phone to ring."

But if you were sending an email or you were corresponding with him each week, and you've provided a written marketing plan upfront, and by the way, one with accountability that's date-specific--and then you go back and if nothing else, each week you're saying, "I committed to mailing a postcard on the 12th and it went out on the 12th. I committed to an email blast on the 15th and gosh, I'm so sorry. I got stuck traveling, but it did go out on the 16th."

If nothing else, if you're providing feedback on what you've done from a marketing perspective, then I'll submit to you that this is 90% of the game.

The other thing is, I don't believe that you've got no activity. You may have no offers, but that doesn't mean that you've had no activity.

You've had people look at the deal. If you'll just take the time to track who's actually looked at the deal, and who's done a tour, when you do your marketing updates include all these individuals. Put the name and the company of the people you've toured. "Gosh, I've done ten tours, and here are all of their names. I've got 75 people who have signed the confidentiality agreement or have registered to look at the offering memorandum. I don't have any offers, but I've got 75 registrations and I've done ten tours, and I've executed on all of the things in the marketing plan that we agreed on upfront. And guess what? We don't have any offers. What do you want to do, Jim?"

That's a whole different conversation than, "Gosh, Jim, I'm sorry we haven't talked in the last 90 days. There's not really much to report. I'm thinking that we should probably lower the price." That owner's going to be like...well, you know what he's going to say!

Jim: Yes, and you could even make them aware of all of the companies you've prospected, too, when you've been making your prospecting calls.

Scott: Sure.

Jim: It shows them you're picking up the phone and dialing, and in addition there are contact management programs today that will help you in tracking all the calls, and help you in sending out all the weekly reports to your owners.

Scott: Yes. There are all kinds of database systems now that allow you to report to your clients on specifically who you've called if you're a technology person.

Jim: You got it. So I know you're someone who's always pushing the envelope and thinking about what the next thing is that you've got to get done. What is it that you think you still need to work on in your own business with your own team to take your brokerage business to the next level?

Scott: It may not be the answer that you're looking for, Jim, but for me I've made some geographic moves. I went from the Dallas market--although I was covering Texas I was primarily in the Dallas market--into management and out to California. I came back and spent just a brief stop in Oklahoma and started some operations there. Then I came back to Texas and I've been back for three years.

In the three years that I've been back I think we've closed about $650 million worth of transactions. But I'm going to tell you that the biggest thing that I need to do is be in my marketplace to the point where I'm the most tenured guy in my marketplace.

At least for one of the two cities, there is an extremely long-term tenured broker who has much more market share than I do. For me to oust him from that post it's going to take some time, and it's going to take a lot of focus on all of the basic blocking and tackling that we've been talking about tonight.

Jim: I understand.

Scott: More than anything else it's about being in one position, and being patient and continuing to chip away and grow my business exponentially each year, until we get to the point where we're number one in market share.

In the other market we're at 30% market share overall, so we're very strong in that market. But I've got a lot of work to do in the other market.

Jim: I understand. We have a question from Neil. Neil, please go ahead and state your question.

Neil: Hi Scott and Jim.

Jim: Hi.

Neil: I had a question and wanted to know what value you would place on specializing in a given market, like a secondary or tertiary market like, say, Tulsa, Oklahoma?

Jim: I think we know who this person is, don't we?

Scott: I think we do.

Jim: For everybody listening, Neil is someone who Scott and I both know, who works in the Tulsa, Oklahoma market. The voice sounded a little bit familiar, and then when you said "Tulsa" I said, "Hold on!" Neil is a great guy, so go ahead and fire away at your answer to that, Scott.

Scott: I'll tell you. If you've got a brain tumor, you're not going to go to a surgeon that does brain surgeries on Tuesdays, knee surgeries on Wednesdays, Thursdays are appendectomies, and Fridays are something else. You're going to go to somebody who does that same type of surgery day-in and day-out; they're going to be a specialist. It's a niche and they're going to be an expert in that field.

I can tell you that my personal track record is roughly $1.5 billion, and in all of that, I've done maybe one single-tenant and one office building that wasn't multi-family. The only reason why I did those two is because I happened to have a private client who was exchanging into a building. Even then, I pulled in an expert on that.

If you're going to want to maximize your revenue, your goal should be to maximize or own market share within a market, and be the foremost expert within that marketplace. It's just that simple. You need to specialize in product, and you need to specialize in market.

Neil: Speaking firsthand, we met when you lived here.

Scott: Yes.

Neil: You know this market specifically. Do you think that it's an excuse that some people use that the market is not big enough to be able to specialize, or does that excuse actually hold water?

Scott: I do think that there are geographic areas where it is difficult to narrowly specialize, but there are ways that you can compensate.

One aspect would be that in a major market like Dallas or Chicago, specialization gets down to the nth degree. You've got people who do nothing but single-tenant net lease, or you've got people who specialize in tenant rep, or you've got agency leasing. Generally speaking, and certainly at the major shops, you'll never have somebody who's just in investment sales. It will be investment sales focused in areas like retail, hospitality, mobile home parks, and multi-family. They're very specialized.

If you're in a small market, you could still leverage. What is specialization, really? It's knowing the buildings, the owners, the transactions, the price points, etcetera. For example, if you're in a small market like Tulsa, maybe you do leasing or tenant rep, or landlord representation and investment sales, but for retail. Or maybe you do all three of those for office.

In my case, when I spent time in Oklahoma, and Neil, as you know, it was strictly multi-family, we just went to a greater geographic area. We went to more of a regional platform versus trying to be just a city platform for my team.

You can do it in different ways. You can scale it in different ways depending on what you're trying to accomplish.

Neil: Based on what you've said tonight, the first thing I'm thinking is that if I've already hired a junior broker, and he's on the call tonight, do you think the next step then would be hiring someone to do back-office work for me?

Scott: There's no question. Again, Neil, I'm willing to bet you that you feel like your time is more valuable than the junior agent who you're training right now. On top of that, if you had two junior agents and you spent all your time going on their appointments, and you're splitting the deal 50/50 with them, now you're still making the exact same amount of money, and you're doing the same amount of deals, but you're helping them to build their business.

Neil: Right.

Scott: You're really not creating leverage. My point is that the first thing you want to do is maximize your own time, which is more valuable right now. At your level of the game you're the senior guy.

Neil: Right.

Scott: First seek to maximize your own revenue-producing activity, and then seek to add fire power.

Neil: Got you.

Jim: Alright.

Neil: Thank you. Maybe we can get out on the golf course where I can maybe win or have some leverage.

Scott: And I've played with Neil before, and yes, he will definitely beat me in golf!

Jim: Actually, let me mention something since Neil stepped up to ask a question. For people who have been a member of this program for some time, they'll remember the story. For people who have come in during the last six months or so, Neil and I have had a coaching relationship together. Neil came to me a couple of years ago and he said, "I've landed this huge opportunity for a tenant rep assignment for office space here in Tulsa. This is something that would be the biggest transaction of the year in our area, but I don't have the resume of transactions in this size range to be able to sit down with the president of the company, the tenant, and be able to say that I'm the best guy for this assignment."

Then I said, "Neil, is there somebody in your territory who has that expertise that you could partner-up with, somebody who you could trust and go after this assignment with together?"

He said, "Yes, I know the perfect guy. He's got a great track record in this arena. He's entrepreneurial. We've done deals together, and he calls his own shots within his own company."

I said, "Approach the guy, generically describing this opportunity to him without telling him who it is, and ask him if he's currently tracking anything like this on his radar screen."

Neil did that, and the guy said, "No."

Then I said, "Approach him about partnering-up." Then they partnered-up on this requirement, they worked it together, and they closed the transaction. So they represented this company together, and Neil ended up walking away with a check for $425,000.00 in commission in his pocket as a direct result of this.

I love that story. It's a great testimonial to somebody like Neil, who is willing to look at out-of-the-box ideas and embrace them, and go for it. I know you got a new car, Neil. "Baby's got new shoes!" Life is better for you now, right?

Neil: Yes. It was a great deal. I learned a lot from it. I built a great relationship and it segued into a great office resume, too. The broker who we partnered-up with on that deal is in his sunset years, especially after we closed that one! He's now slowly transferring things over to us, and putting a good word in as he's transferring over his clients.

Now it seems like with the things that we've already put in place in our office, it's a natural transition into doing office specialization. It's something that I've got a lot of experience in, and I've done it both nationwide and internationally. It seems like now is the time, and Scott's right...people want to work with a specialist.

Scott: I'll put it to you this way. My former company has a couple of retail brokers who are perennial top ten brokers. They built their practices and they became top ten brokers in the firm. It's a big, national firm with the largest sales force in the country for investment sales only, and these guys are constantly in the top ten. The reason is they specialize. One of them does strip centers. The other one does single-tenant net lease, but that guy does transactions nationally. He's in one geographic location, and he's national.

I had another guy who I coached. He was one of my agents when I was a manager out in Encino, California, who does single-tenant net lease primarily, and he grew his business nationally. He was able to move from California to the East Coast without disrupting his business at all, and that's one example of specialization.

There are certain guys who specialize in just Walgreens, or in certain leases. They can really get narrow in their specialization.

One company's platform has a tax credit team out of the Pacific Northwest and they're the most dominant in their space. You could take all the other major brokerage shops and take their tax credit teams and put them on one team and their volume would be less than this tax credit team. They're all in one office in the Pacific Northwest.

So with specialization in certain product types like multi-family, you can't cover too much dirt in multi-family. In retail, you can. In office, I don't know. I don't have the expertise to know whether or not you should attempt to do that in office. Everything is just a little bit different. But for sure, product specialty is a no-brainer.

Jim: Alright.

Neil: Thank you, guys.

Jim: Scott, do you have time for one more question if we've got one?

Scott: Sure.

Jim: We have another question from David. David, please go ahead.

David: Hey, I've got a question for you. The last hour and a half went really quick because you're really good, and I really appreciate everything you've said. And thanks, Jim, for having him on.

Scott, I listed the back office people that you've got. You've got graphics, analytics, admin, research, finance, marketing, driver, and lead generator. If you're starting a full back office like that, what would you suggest would be the priority in terms of which one of those you would hire, and in what order in terms of importance?

Scott: Two things come into mind. First, start with roles, not people or bodies. Not many people on the call can drop a six or seven-person back-office team in place all at once and financially handle that. It's not about the number of bodies.

We're to the point where we have individual bodies for those different roles, but that's not to say that when you're first starting out that your financial analyst might not also be doing the research piece of it. Your administrative assistant might be doing the marketing. Or, in the very beginning, it's just one person wearing a lot of different hats.

The other thing you have to look at is where you are spending your time in non-revenue-producing activity. I'm going to guess that your time will get wrapped up in pushing the marketing out, and in managing the escrows. Those are going to be the two biggest time consumers of non-revenue-producing activity.

Your goal should be to hire somebody who is intelligent and capable enough, and has the aptitude to be able to manage those processes in such a way that you get your time back. So think about it in terms of roles, not the number of bodies.

David: Being a broker here with several agents, one of the things that I need to do, for example, is on a purchase agreement or a lease, I always want to look at that before it goes out for signature from a liability standpoint. I want to make sure it's correct, and that there's another set of eyes that have seen it, so we don't have egg on our face if it comes back because we've done something wrong.

If you have a contract go out, a purchase in your case, do you read it and approve it before it goes out for signature?

Scott: Good question. On the private side, yes. On the major asset side, no, because my clients sometimes have in-house counsel, and they'll all have outsource counsel. So a lot of times I'm not involved with the legal aspect at all. On the private side, it's certainly where I' beginning, when I was doing primarily private, we d legal documents.

We talked about systems and processes, and we actually built a database for the transactions. Once we took our firm's legal document, we would enter the information into a database one time, and then we could mail-merge it into our legal forms. So the owner information, the legal entity, the purchase price, and all that stuff would be generated. You would go back, and, for example, after you did it the first time and you then have to do a Receipt of Documents, or you have to do an amendment or an addendum, all that was system-generated directly out of a database, because we entered it one time. That was a time-leverage thing.

The answer is yes. My staff would draft it and I would review it. If you look at my calendar right now, you'll see that every night from 8:00 p.m. to 9:00 p.m. is workout, and from 9:00 p.m. to 10:00 p.m. is review. I literally sit with my iPad, and there's a great app I utilize called Notes Plus.

David: OK.

Scott: Now I get all of my cash flow models, my offering memorandums, proposals, and legal documents emailed to me by my staff, and I flag them for homework. From 9:00 p.m. to 10:00 p.m. each night I pull out my iPad, and I open up Notes Plus. I pull the document up as a PDF in Notes Plus, and I can write on the screen, and I can email it directly back to people. I don't even have to print out the documents anymore.

David: OK.

Scott: I chalk it up and make notes, and I reply, and I push it back out to them via email. Then they'll send it back to me again the next day for me to review at night, and we'll do this until it's completed and sent out.

bviously, if there's something with critical timing you can do that during the day, but even if I'm sitting in the office and my assistant is right across from me, I'm still going to get an email. I'm still going to do that review on my tablet, and it's going to go right back to them without ever having been printed out.

David: And obviously, that's a non-revenue producing activity, and like you said, it occurs between 9:00 p.m. and 10:00 p.m. at night.

Scott: Correct, and on top of that, remember when I said I only want to be CEO for 15 minutes a day? I'm not giving up accountability for my team. Everything that goes out, every marketing piece, every offering memorandum, every proposal, every cash flow model, and every legal document has my eyes on it before it goes out. But I want to spend the least amount of time as humanly possible on this. So my back-office people are specialized. My financial analyst is doing the same cash flow model over and over again. They know what kind of assumptions I'm going to expect, etcetera. They know I'm going to chalk it up and send it back to them, and they'll keep getting the revisions until it's done.

But I'm not going to do the legwork. I'm not going to do the first pass at the investment drivers. I'm not going to write up the investment summary. I'm not going to draft up the PSA. I'm not going to draft the amendment. I'm not going to itemize the due diligence documents. All of that is going to be managed by somebody in my back office, and I'm just going to approve it.

David: Got it. Terrific! Thanks for your help.

Jim: Thanks for your question, too, David.

David: OK, guys. Take care.

Jim: So in moving forward, Scott, thank you so much for being here with us tonight, man. You're a wonderful guy, and you've got such great information. Is there anything you want to say as we're moving forward towards completion here?

Scott: I just want to give one last little tip, and that is to check out a website called www.Stickk.com. This is a website where you can create a personal contract with yourself, put your credit card up, and you can set a goal in there. You can have a coach. Jim could be your coach, and part of your weekly session with Jim could be that he can check and approve if you've completed your goal or not. In addition, you could also have somebody else in your office be your coach.

You submit a goal, you put a credit card up, and you choose the amount. It's an accountability system such that if you miss your goal, your credit card is automatically charged, and it goes either to a charity, to an anti-charity, to a competitor, or to a friend. You choose where the money goes, but it's a great, great accountability system. I challenge you to take one area of your business that you need to improve on the most, create a goal, put some money on the line, and then create a personal contract.

Jim: That's a great resource that I've utilized with some of my coaching clients, too. Sometimes, when I work with brokers who keep on missing their prospecting numbers, I tell them to make an agreement with themselves to make a contribution to a charity that they believe in at the end of the week if they continue missing their prospecting numbers, but this now takes it up to an entirely new level, to be able to actually go to a website like this and set it all up.

There was one of my coaching clients, a guy who, after 14 years in the business, was grossing $200,000.00 to $300,000.00 in commissions per year, and then within just several years, we got him up to grossing $1,400,000.00 in commissions per year. When I was working with him with this concept, I told him to pay the money to his #1 rival in the office, a guy that he didn't like at all. But when I suggested this to him, he came back to me with, "Over my dead body!!!", and I knew that we had established the right kind of motivation.

But still, he didn't want to ever put himself in that position, so we had him pay the money to a charity that he believed in instead.

With this in mind, this now completes our teleconference. Thanks to everyone for being on the call with us, and thanks again, Scott, for taking the time to be with us.

INTERVIEW 5

Beating Your Commercial Real Estate Competitors for the Business

Jim: Hi, this is Jim Gillespie, America's Premier Commercial Real Estate Coach[sm] located on the web at www.CommercialRealEstateCoach.com. Today I am going to be interviewing our special guest, Bill Gladstone of NAI CIR, and then at the end of my interview with Bill we're going to take your questions on anything you'd like to know to help you to take your commercial brokerage business to the next level.

We will be going in total for approximately one hour and thirty minutes tonight, and with that being said, let me get into an introduction for Bill:

Bill Gladstone, CCIM and SIOR, works with NAI CIR in Harrisburg, Pennsylvania, and he's been active in commercial and industrial real estate since 1987. Over the years he has typically overseen the marketing for a revolving inventory of more than 130 listings, he maintains an annual average of $40 million in transaction volume, and at any moment in time he is typically the exclusive listing agent for approximately one million square feet of office, industrial, warehouse, and commercial space, as well as 100-125 acres of land.

He has chosen a niche for his business model and stays within that model to continually achieve success as a landlord or seller's broker. He has a team of five people, including himself, and each person on his team has a specific job function with little or no duplication of effort, which makes this model both very efficient and very profitable for him.

With all that being said, Bill, thanks so much for being with us. Welcome onto the call.

Bill: Thank you, Jim. It's a pleasure being with you.

Jim: When you and I were getting ready for this call over the last several days, you mentioned to me how you've gotten involved in some national relationships with some major companies in your brokerage business. I wanted to have you talk for a moment about this and have you tell us about these opportunities, and what this actually creates for you in terms of even more opportunities for you in your brokerage business.

Bill: Sure, Jim, I'd be glad to. When we talked about it, I always think about how you can be creative and how you can do something different that your competition isn't doing. A lot of it just goes back to very simple stuff. You work well with people. Sometimes you ask them if you can help them anyplace else, and sometimes they need the help, and if you do a good job, it grows.

I've had two opportunities like that. One is with Santander Bank. They take back REO properties, and they had somehow contacted me about this originally. I had done one deal with them because it was right here in my market, and then they started to go around the country.

For those of you who may not be familiar with Santander, that is the Spanish bank. I believe they are the fourth largest bank in the world. They rank up in the top, but they have a lot of REO--Real Estate Owned--here in the states. Wherever there was a Sovereign Bank before, that is now Santander, just by way of explanation.

They have a lot of REO, and at anytime and at any given point this grew to about eleven deals. I mean, you could call me up and I could go through probably ten to eleven deals, maybe twelve deals, where we were doing deals in Dallas, New Jersey, Pennsylvania, and a number of different states.

As we did that, it was not selling real estate so much as managing brokers who are selling real estate. After that, I started working with a trucking company, J.B. Hunt. I don't have an exclusive with them, but they call me regularly. I got a call today to help them on a lease because we've established such a good working relationship, and that came from a deal we had put together up here. We sold on an old Roadway terminal which we knocked down, and they built a maintenance shop since they really didn't need the terminal.

We worked well together and I said, "Can I help you anyplace else?" We had just finished up a deal in Ayer, Massachusetts. We're working on a deal right now in Greencastle, Pennsylvania. We've done a number of other deals where I've found brokers and managed the brokers for them, so they only had one point of contact, which was me, and they kind of liked that. It lessens the load, and he gets his work done faster, so it's worked out well.

What that has done is, instead of actually selling the real estate, is it's just managing the brokers. I think this past year, net to me, J.B. Hunt was somewhere around $8,000.00 for phone calls. I think Santander was somewhere around $12,000.00. So it's a total of $20,000.00. You can't live on that, but it's certainly $20,000.00 that wasn't there the year before, and the amount of time I put into it was maybe five hours on a deal. Some deals involved very little time, and some deals maybe a little more time. In all, it hasn't been a lot of time.

It's a nice niche. In the sale of the real estate it's a nice niche, and it gets back to what you and I were talking about: find your niche, whether it's in real estate or whether it's in the marketing of the real estate.

Jim: I think you mentioned, at least with one of the companies, aren't you now in a position to handle almost everything nationally for them, at least maybe in terms of the selection of the brokerage companies that might be working on the transactions?

Bill: Yes, in both cases. They just say, "Find a broker." So I do. I can go to the NAI system, I can go to the SIOR system, or I can go to the CCIM system. All they want is results, and they want to know that you're being honest and fair with them.

Over time you create your credibility. More and more they just say, "Go ahead and do it. Get it done and we're happy." That's what it takes.

Jim: You mentioned to me when we were talking about this several days ago that if you could have a few more of these relationships, basically that would allow you to generate an extremely solid amount of income for a lot less work in your brokerage business, right?

Bill: Oh, absolutely. And combined with the real estate brokerage business, it's what I would consider gravy. This is the extra you get for being a good boy and paying attention. You know, $20,000.00 is not a lot of money for a lot of brokers, but it's $20,000.00 I didn't have the year before.

Jim: But it's something where I'm guessing that you can see the path that this can go down in terms of building more solid relationships with these people, to get a lot more business from the relationship.

Bill: From that relationship, and hopefully to bring it into other relationships.

I was with a convenience chain this morning, and they only have 60 stores, and they want to accelerate growth and it's regional, but we're talking about the same thing because I don't want to travel. I like to stay in my market. I'm a landlord or a seller's broker because I have a great marketing system, at least I think I have a good marketing system, and so I don't want to be spread out too thin.

I proposed to them that I could manage brokers for them in areas that I choose not to work in, not because I'm lazy, but because I don't think it's in their best interest to have me traveling the highways instead of doing what I do well for them in my market, and then I'll put a team together of other brokers.

We've already done that in certain areas with them. It's just now they want to try to formalize it, and they're trying to see what the best way to do it is. It's a beauty contest. I'm in the lineup and I've got a track record with them.

Jim: One of the things that we're going to get into here tonight is the kind of marketing that you do, which is the best marketing that I've ever seen done in commercial real estate brokerage. I wanted to ask you, in whatever you were doing before you ever got into commercial real estate brokerage, did you see things going on that had you go, "Wait a second. Nobody is doing this type of marketing in commercial real estate brokerage. I bet if I took what I see working successfully over here and brought it over to commercial real estate brokerage, I bet I could make big things happen?"

I'm just curious if you noticed things outside of brokerage that had you say, "Boy, this would carry over well if I become the only guy that I know of doing something like this."

Bill: Great question, and the answer is "yes", I did see something. I translated that for myself into a concept. The concept is, when times get tough and everybody wants to cut costs, be the maverick. Be the lone person. Go out on a limb and say, "I'm not going to cut costs; I'm going to increase sales." Nobody else is doing that.

I'll give you a prime example. I was in the restaurant business immediately before I got into real estate. The one restaurant I was working in, the order came down from up top because it was a chain restaurant and I was actually at the training center training managers.

The order came down, "You've got to cut your costs. We've got to improve the bottom line."

I thought about it and I said, "You know, let's try to increase the sales." One of the things I was thinking about, and it was a beef house at that time, was we had an eight-ounce cut of prime rib. It was the petite cut. What I did was, and there were other examples like this, but let's just focus on one, because you'll get the hang of it if I just go over one.

I took the eight-ounce cut and I cut it back to six ounces. I wrapped it in a puff pastry dough. Then when you put that in the convection oven and it blows up, it fills up more than half the plate. By the time you put a vegetable on there, and by the time you put a garnish on there, and a potato, everything is hanging over the edge so to speak. It looks huge!

We increased the price by $2.50 a plate. So we cut it by two ounces and we increased the price by $2.50, and we sold out of them every time we had them on the menu!

You're not going to be able to wake up every morning and say, "Aha! I have this thought, and this is what I'm going to do." We got lucky with a few of these things and it transcended into increasing the sales as opposed to just focusing on, "Let's cut the dishwasher back an hour and a half. Let's do this and make it a little bit more painful for everybody." We didn't have to do that.

I never forgot that, and I'll never forget some of the other examples I had with that. As I moved into real estate I said, "Let's try to be a little bit contrary." If everybody says, "Right," let's say, "Left," and see what happens. That's how this whole concept of the marketing program that you and I have talked about over the years emerged.

Jim: Why is marketing so important in commercial real estate brokerage, and why aren't many people doing it?

Bill: To me, Jim, it's so important because it differentiates you from your competition. If you can differentiate yourself from your competition, you have just blown your competition away, because that's what they're trying to do to you, but they haven't done it.

You need to be the first one out there to do it. Think of something dramatic, think of something different, and it can be simple. When I first did this, it was simple. The reason that you do this is you need to be able to differentiate yourself.

Why don't people do it? It comes back to money. I've been doing this for 27 years, and even the brokers in my own firm--and I was like that until I trained myself not to be like that--do not want to spend money.

Do you know when they spend money? It's when they've made a commission and they have money in their pocket. Then they say, "OK, I'll go out and spend some of this." They won't spend much, but they'll spend some of it.

I'm saying to change your thinking. Spend the money to make the money. Differentiate yourself from your competition and stay focused, and you'll keep on going down that path which will take you to the success that you really want to have.

Jim: Absolutely, and just with you saying that right there, brokers are so conditioned into not spending money until they get it. That fits in perfectly with the paradigm that they work under, where normally they're working in a brokerage office, and they have no out-of-pocket monthly expenses for anything. The rent for the office is paid for, the phones, the receptionist, the admin people. Unlike normal business owners, like someone who would own a restaurant or a dry cleaners, they're not used to spending money on an ongoing basis, regardless of what the cash flow is for them in any given month.

That feeds perfectly into developing an attitude of, "I don't spend money except for my normal personal expenses. But when the check comes, now I've got some additional walking around money." Oftentimes, though, that still doesn't translate into spending any money on marketing.

Bill: No, unfortunately, and you've brought up a very good point. You said that they don't run it like a business, and that was a key turning point for me.

Well, what I decided to do several years ago was I said, "Here's what I'm going to do." I now report my checks to my accountant for what I've made every two weeks when I get paid. I send all my receipts to the accountant, and the only receipts that I send are the receipts that are business-related. If it's not business-related, even if I go out for dinner with some friends and it looks like it could have been entertainment, and I could justify talking about real estate, I don't, because that wasn't the purpose.

I actually have them generate every month a P&L for me that shows me where I am year-to-date, where I compare year-to-date to the year before, and it shows how I'm tracking so far for the year. So I can tell you at any given point where I am and where I expect to be for the rest of the year.

Now you're really running this as a business. So when you sit down and you see those numbers, and you see that sales aren't good, you could say, "Cut your costs." On the other hand, you could say, "What can I do? What can I do to spend money to increase my sales so that I can make more money?" That's a personal choice. Some people are comfortable with it and some people won't be.

If you like to take a challenge, I suggest that this is a challenge you might want to consider.

Jim: I think one of the biggest reframes mentally that brokers need to make is around this idea that spending money on marketing is just an expense. It's cash out-of-pocket. They can't see where it's going to lead to in terms of more business coming in as a result of the outlay of cash, and it's very difficult for them oftentimes to get over the idea of that initial cash outflow. Also, they look around the office and say, "Well, nobody else in my office is doing anything like this, so clearly it must not work. Therefore, I shouldn't be spending any money on marketing either."

Don't you find that this is kind of a circular way of thinking? Based upon what they see in the office, I can see why they would conclude that, but it's basically moving them at light speed to remaining exactly where they are right now in their brokerage production and revenue, right?

Bill: Absolutely. It's the path of least resistance, but if you said, "Would you like to take the path of least resistance, or would you like to make more money than you ever thought possible?", what do you think they would say there? I mean, that is a choice. As a 1099 businessperson, that is what you do; you make choices.

It's a personal decision, and sometimes it's very easy because of the situation you're in. I know that for a fact, because when I first got into real estate, I was broke. I mean, it was embarrassing. I hated to go home at night. I worked from eight in the morning until eight at night, or nine at night if I could, and I had no money, and nothing to show for it. My mortgage was due, I had three kids who were younger then with a lot of expenses. I had my wife, two car payments, a house payment, and she wasn't working. So I know what it's like.

It's a very painful experience, but I chose to take the challenge, and I never want to go back to that horrible little place. That keeps me focused.

I can imagine there are a lot of people who you coach who are in that same position, and some people, unfortunately, will probably stay there because they don't want to take the challenge. Some people will take your advice and they will move on, and they will accelerate, and they will be really proud of themselves and pleased with what they were able to accomplish.

Jim: I find, oftentimes along those lines, Bill, that so many people elevate themselves to their own specific level of financial stress, just because of how they're playing the game.

I look at some of these people who I know have $50,000.00 a month mortgage payments, and I'm thinking, "Do you think that they ever experience stress financially?"

I mean, you look at their amazing house and you go, "Wow! That's phenomenal, but how much must the payments be on this thing?" I'm sure the cash flow gets a little tight from time-to-time and they're feeling stress at their own level, just like somebody trying to come up with hundreds of dollars for their car payment every month.

Bill: Absolutely.

Jim: You talked about the importance of differentiation and standing out, and I wholeheartedly agree, but I find that so many brokers rely on prospecting to develop more new business for themselves. But oftentimes they're not getting their prospecting done as they'd like to, and at the same time, you can't really differentiate yourself and stand out from the pack if you're relying on prospecting, but not doing any great marketing along with it, right?

Bill: Very true.

Jim: How do you differentiate yourself when all of your competitors are making the same kinds of prospecting calls? You're dialing out, you're not meeting the person face-to-face, they say they're not ready to do anything for six months, you make a note to call them in another two to four months, or something like that, and all of your competitors will be doing the same.

By the time you're talking to them again, do you think you're really standing out and differentiating yourself when you're just talking to them on the phone, while all of your other competitors are doing the exact same thing? I don't think so.

Bill: Not at all. People used to tell me, "Stay with the basics. Stay with the basics." I've been in this business for 27 years, so I remember being thrown into a room and them telling me, "Here's a phone book. Go to work."

I was thinking, "What kind of training is that?"

Jim: It's the typical training in our industry, unfortunately.

Bill: Yes. We don't do training in this industry as well as we could, or as well as we should.

I thought about this because I was getting ready for this call for the past month or so; it's just one of those things. I don't do any prospecting, and I'm always afraid when I wake up in the morning thinking, "I should probably do some prospecting, because that's a basic." People have always told me this, and it was ingrained in me to stick to the basics.

My business now is by word-of-mouth, referral business, or repeat business. That's it. I don't prospect. It's not that I don't want to, but I don't have time.

This year, unfortunately, as you and I were discussing in one conversation, I came in as number two in the office. The first guy blew everybody away. He had some really great industrial renewals and they were just huge, and there was no way to compete with that this year.

Jim: Bill, since you and I were chatting about that before we actually kicked off the call tonight, why don't you mention, just for everybody listening, what the guy made in the first quarter?

Bill: Oh, they had a luncheon the other day and they said in the first quarter it was the most money they had ever paid an agent in a single year. I looked back to some of my best years, and in a small market, and this attests to my marketing, too, the City of Harrisburg, Pennsylvania is a city with 48,000 people. If you take what I call a local SMA, the two counties surrounding the city have 250,000 people each for a total of 500,000. Take out the farmers and everybody else who are not involved, and you probably have about 300,000 people in my market and that's it.

But in my best year ever, I think I made $1,110,000.00. So that guy in the first quarter made more than $1.1 million.

Jim: Wow!

Bill: I don't know what he did the rest of the year because, again, those were renewals, but I don't think you have to do too much the rest of the entire year, do you?

Jim: No, but you just reminded me of another story that I just want to mention here. There was one time when I was managing an office, and a broker in the office basically kicked off the year by getting a $440,000.00 commission. Unfortunately, the rest of the year he just kept coming in and kicking up his feet on the desk all the time, and walking around and wasting the time of the other brokers.

Basically, after a period of time, I finally let him go. I said, "Look, you've got to be more productive than just sitting around and doing this."

He was just being a pain. It was basically a company in a situation where we were all shareholders in the company together, so he was spending time going over all the financial statements and trying to figure out how he could change how we divide all the profits, to put another ten grand in his pocket at the end of the year. So I'm telling him, "Why don't you just go out and try to make another ten grand instead of figuring out how you can take it from everybody else?"

You're right. When something like that happens in the early part of the year, you can all of a sudden kick back if you don't watch it.

That's a huge number that guy you mentioned made in the first quarter. That's awesome!

Bill: My business model is built on mid-sized deals. I don't do the whale hunts like that other fellow does. I mean, he's out with the big box warehouses. I'm more of a generalist, and my commissions usually range somewhere in the $30's, the $40's, the $50's, and the $60's, and lower, too, with the small deals. That's the market I try to attract.

I can have a good year, not a great year, but a good year every year because I can make those kinds of deals somewhere.

You go out and you try to pick up a half million-dollar fee, or a $750,000.00 to $1 million fee, and those aren't always out there. You're living on the edge. You can have a great year or you can have a really poor year.

My model is different. I wished him well and I was glad he was able to do that, but he's only been number one once before in the company maybe ten years ago.

Jim: So you're really glad that this is a new year, so that you get another crack with a clean slate at being number one again, right?

Bill: Oh, absolutely. Who likes to go to a lunch and say, "I'm the first loser." No way!

Jim: Miss Congeniality, right?

Bill: Yes.

Jim: Basically, nobody ever thought their entire life and said, "Boy, I really want to be the second-best at what I do."

Bill: I agree.

Jim: Wouldn't you agree that when you're mailing to your people and you're sending them videos of you to watch, basically educating them on what is going on in the marketplace, that it's similar in many ways to getting face-to-face time with them, which actually helps to create a deeper bond with them? Would you agree with that?

Bill: Absolutely on that one, too. Yes.

The thing about the videos is they came from something else. I think what they came from was they evolved from the CDs, and the CDs came from the PowerPoints, or vice-versa. Everything trickles back, Jim, to the one-page newsletter that I remember I started with.

I remember I took one page with two sides. If it's a trifold, you have six panels. If you put a header on one that says, "Hi, this is my newsletter," and you put an address on another, you've only got four panels left to work with. One page and a third is what you've got left.

The bottom line is: What is the most important thing you can do with that one page and a third that you have left? I always figured I would put my picture on there, too.

I did a newsletter. It was rough paper. It was two-color. It was probably poor, but my picture went across everybody's desk that I sent it to every month. I had a picture on their desk every month. Even if they didn't read it, I wanted them to pick it up, see the name Bill Gladstone, and see my picture, and then throw it away if they didn't want to read it. Quite frankly,

I don't know if they read it or not, but that evolved into videos for me. It evolved into a magazine. It's evolved into a four-color, eight-page newsletter now.

You build off of that, and I would encourage the people you are talking to right now, that if they've ever done this before, yes, focus on the video, but gradually take yourself to that video by starting smaller with a traditional-type thing. Start with a one-page newsletter if you're not doing a newsletter. If you're doing a newsletter, try to enhance it. Do whatever you can to build towards doing that video.

The video has to be very specific. You and I talked about that a little bit offline, too. It just can't be, "Oh, let's do a video," and you put something up there. Just because it's a video doesn't mean it's going to work.

We have our own equipment. We have a green screen, and we have a video recorder. We have bought a lot of equipment over the years, because I have four assistants and one of them is my Marketing Director. She knows how to use all of that stuff, and we'll do stuff with it, but you really have to follow certain parameters of the industry. Until you get those down and right, and to be honest with you we haven't, your videos are going to suffer.

Rather than waiting for you to get that right, in the meantime build and go forward by using something as simple as a newsletter, something that has your picture on it that goes across the desk. That will help create the bond, too. That will help them to say, "Oh, yes. I get your newsletter." Or, "I think I get your newsletter."

That's all you need is some encouragement, and then help them along so that you can then say, "Yes, you do get my newsletter," and you can take it from there so they at least have something in common with you, a bond of some sort, when you're talking to them on the phone or when you're sitting in their office.

Jim: I think it's so great to hear you talk about the importance of including your photo on your mailers, because so many commercial brokers say, "Wait a second. That's what those residential agents do, and I'm a commercial person. I don't want to do anything that may look like I'm a residential agent." That's a huge marketing mistake, isn't it?

Bill: I think so, yes. They feel closer to you when you include your photo.

It's like when you look at LinkedIn and there's a blank space there. I always feel lonely. It's like my picture is out there. You can get to my screen. You've obviously been there because you're asking me to connect with you. I get to your screen, and I can read about you and I can do all these things, but I can't see you.

It's OK. I understand, and I accept the invitation if I like the bio and I go for it, but it would be so much nicer just to have a picture of that person, because it could be so much more meaningful than just having to read the text.

Jim: You're right. When you see that blank space, it's almost like the person has left their body or something like that. It's just empty. You can't really have that feeling of connecting with a human being in this situation, and that is something that including your photos does.

The people may have never spoken with you before. They may have never met you face-to-face, but now there is this feeling that they have some kind of relationship with you, because they see what you look like visually.

I remember one time, this one broker told me something that happened to him. This was a very successful SIOR broker, and I kept coaching him on including his photos within his mailers. He finally started doing this, and then he said, "Now I'm like a celebrity when I walk into people's offices. They say, 'You're the guy who's been sending us the mailers, and it's great to finally meet you!'"

They began recognizing him because of his photos, and he now kind of walks in their door being a semi-celebrity. You can't do that when you don't include your photos on your mailers.

Bill: Right.

Jim: You've just got to do it because it's good marketing. It doesn't matter what the residential people do. It's good marketing. And quite honestly, when it comes to technology, the residential agents have been far ahead of the commercial agents for a long time, and it's still rare to have a broker have his or her own standalone agent website in commercial real estate brokerage right now. That's just the way it is.

Bill: Yes.

Jim: Why don't you tell us about your mailing program? Tell us what you're mailing to your clients and prospects, and how often you're doing it.

Bill: OK. We break it up into four types of marketing, and they overlap. One is traditional marketing, where we send stuff out on paper. One is digital marketing, where it all goes electronic. The other is what we call object marketing, where I have a breakfast coming up and I have a table. We will have something there for them. We have kind of a neat gadget; it's a paperclip. We have our own bottled water. We have our own T-shirts. They will be wrapped up nicely and they'll be in front of everybody's place when they get there to the breakfast, an economic forecast breakfast. It will be the only table that has that stuff, or has anything other than a seat for the person to sit down and start talking, because most people don't think ahead like that. Again, it's a way to differentiate yourself.

We think carefully and clearly about things like that, but this would be object marketing. Then we do a lot of personal marketing, and there is an overlap here. I'm at a table with seven people, carefully picked so that no field is overlapping. I have an engineer, I have an attorney, we have an architect, we have a businessperson who does retail sales, and a few others in other categories so that I'm able to market to them.

The nice thing about this economic forecast breakfast is that this guy, with the financial institution he's with, has written for my magazine, which is something we'll get back to shortly.

We try to encompass all of those and look for ideas and avenues to say, "Hey, this is the Bill Gladstone Group and we'd love to work with you. This is how we market not only ourselves, but this is an example or a concept of how we would handle your property for you." People get very comfortable with that, because they can actually see what we do, but we do have four different ways of doing it.

When we go to the traditional side of it, the two key pieces for us are our newsletter, which we used to do in a green shell with black and white. It was OK, but it wasn't anything outstanding. It got our face out there, and that was what we wanted it to do. That was when it went out to about 4,000 people.

Interestingly enough, when you talk about spending money, when times got tough during the last downturn I said to my group, "You know, we need to really think about how to differentiate ourselves because these are tough times. We need to spend money if we're going to make money."

We put our heads together and we came up with an $800.00 a month newsletter and turned it into a four-color, eight-page newsletter. We moved the price from $800.00 a month to $1,700.00 a month, but it's a beautiful piece. I mean it shines, and nobody else is doing it, because nobody wants to spend the money, especially back then because the economy was tough.

That goes out to 4,000 people, and it has a picture of our group on it. It also has my picture on it, it's very specifically designed to market us, and it goes out monthly. Write these numbers down: that's $1,700.00 times twelve during the year.

To go along with that, then we send out our magazine. Our magazine definitely differentiates ourselves from all the others, because there is no other real estate magazine in this market. That also goes out to about 4,000 people.

The magazine is quarterly. It's 44 pages, and four-color. We do sell ads in there, and we've hired a lady who is a 1099 person to sell the ads for us. Each copy of the magazine costs $3.75. If you want to translate that into 4,000 copies four times a year, it's about $60,000.00. So it costs $15,000.00 every time an issue comes out.

When the economy is tough, I'm not getting $15,000.00 from the people who choose to advertise in there, and I have to make up the difference. But if you took a look at the people who advertise in this magazine, and keep in mind, don't go to sleep tonight and say, "I'm going to do a magazine tomorrow because it sounds like a great idea, and Bill did it." It took us years to develop this, and we started with a newsletter, and then we moved into the magazine because we wanted to be different.

We have people writing articles. We have four articles in there that are 1,600 words each. Some of the furniture people advertise in there, and some of the law firms advertise in there. I leave it all up to this young lady. She's very good at what she does, and she sells the advertising.

It's worked out pretty well, but again, we're always on the cover. You received the last one, Jim, where the editorial was about goal setting. I was on the cover with a score sheet. It looked like we were doing football plays, and we try to match the cover to the editorial.

We've done a number of things. For example, pictures from high atop buildings, but my picture is always on the cover of that magazine, so that when it comes in people say, "Oh, that's that guy who is always sending us stuff," or something like that, so I can get some recognition having spent that kind of money for this magazine.

Jim: It's a phenomenal publication, the magazine. It's just beautiful and glossy. It's along the lines in both the size and the number of pages of CCIM's magazine, or the SIOR Professional Report. It's just so beautifully and professionally done.

You'll have articles by people in there like CPAs, attorneys, title people, and people with businesses in your area...basically real estate-related articles from people that your clients and prospects might want to hear from. You've got so many different contributors to it as well as the advertisers, and it's just a phenomenal publication.

Bill: We're very fortunate because we learned how to grow it, and it's not just about real estate. We had a chiropractor write an article, because so many people sit at their desks and they have neck pain. We explained this to them, and even with my staff I send them to a chiropractor every once in a while, just to get adjusted so they feel a little better, because they spend eight hours a day at a computer staring at a screen.

For your health, that's probably not the best thing, but that's such a relevant topic. We can relate it to real estate...people sitting at desks, people who are decision makers, or whatever. We got some calls back on that one, and it was pretty good.

We try to vary it as much as possible, and it really is a nice publication, but we worked hard to get it to that.

That goes out quarterly, so another 4,000 people are touched on a quarterly basis, for a total of at least twice a month every three months, including all of the publications that they receive from us. We do flyers. We only do flyers to very targeted audiences. We do touch people with the flyers, and we do postcards. We like to do postcards, because we find that if you can do a little bit of humor in your postcard, people will at least look at the front of it, and they will flip it over before they throw it away.

Sometimes when the flyer comes in the envelope, if they see it's from a realty company, or it looks like it might not be something they're really interested in, they'll just pitch it. They may not even open the envelope. We're careful about that, but those are the ways that we try to touch our clients.

At this point, we've tried other things, too, where we've tried to get special mailings out, including trifold postcards, but we really didn't get much out of those. We tried to vary things that were on each panel of the postcards. We've done a number of different things like that, but basically, I think we're down to our basics, from a traditional standpoint, of using the magazine, the flyers, the newsletter, and postcards.

From a digital standpoint, we have our website. We don't like using email much anymore, because I find myself just deleting them. I try to get them out of my inbox, because right now, in sitting sit here and talking to you, I'm in trouble. I've got over 600 emails in my inbox, and I struggle with it every day. I'll stay up late tonight to try to delete 100 of them, and then 150 of them will come in tomorrow.

It's not so much spam because I've got a good spam filter, but some of them just need to be filed. Some of them do need to be responded to, but I don't want this to be an annoyance. I don't want someone to say, "Oh, that's Gladstone again, ugh!" I don't want them to have that feeling about me. I want them to feel good whenever I contact them, so I do stay away from that.

Jim: You bring up an important point. You said you don't want them to perceive that you're an annoyance to them, and we're talking about them receiving both email and mailers from you.

Why don't you talk for a moment about how sending them quality mailers with good information about what's going on in your marketplace, or sending them things that they'll want to know about through the mail--why this is more OK and not nearly as much of an interruption as them receiving email from you.

Bill: I think one of the things is that the mailers don't come in with such abundance like the emails do. I mean, it's hard to control those emails. They just keep flowing in.

When the mail comes at noon, usually it's just a handful. A lot of times the secretary can just control that and sort it out. By the time it gets to your desk, there are a couple of magazines, and there might be a couple of letters that have already been opened up for you, so you don't have to go through the time it takes to open the letters. It's just very easy with mail.

It's not so easy with emails, because they come right to your inbox and you're inundated. It just doesn't stop. I think that's one of the problems with email. I look at my inbox and I try to imagine other people who might be having the same reaction as me. I say, "Gee, why do they keep sending me this stuff? I don't want it. I don't want it," and yet it still shows up. It's something I'm totally not interested in, but it shows up. Or, if it is something I'm interested in, it's offered in such a bland way showing that this person doesn't really know me, and that they don't care about me. They just have a product and they're trying to sell it to me.

That's the way I look at it, and I think other people do, too.

Jim: I think also when email is coming in, in the midst of people dealing with all of the spam simultaneously, there can be such a feeling of overwhelm, and your email and message can be associated with that feeling, including all of the spam. This isn't good when compared to what you were just talking about with something coming in the mail...with just five or ten pieces coming in a given day. Then when you add to this the fact that what you're sending them in the mail looks nice and glossy, there's a certain perception of you being a true professional, because you're willing to spend that kind of money. But anyone can just click and send an email, and so many people do, because it's basically free. That really helps to set you apart and differentiate you, too...agreed?

Bill: Absolutely, yes.

Jim: So mail is a tremendous way to brand yourself in people's minds. But so many brokers, when they start to think about doing mail, they start thinking automatically of minimizing the cost. So don't do it on the cheap, because it's going to create a cheap impression of you when it's received.

Make it look classy. Spend the money, because that's the image they are going to have of you when they receive your mailer. You don't want them to begin thinking of you as being cheap through your marketing, because people don't want to work with cheap brokers. If you're going to send out cheap mailers, you'd be better off not sending them out at all, because you don't want to create this impression of yourself in people's minds.

Bill: Yes, and to the point with the magazine, I get so many comments from people who say, "Didn't I just see you on the cover of a magazine?"

Then I say, "Yes."

They say, "Wow! How do you do that?"

So I say, "Well, I print the magazine myself."

It's kind of humorous because they thought maybe it was on some special publication, but they remember the face. They remember the face when they see me, and that's what I'm looking for. I'm trying to get them to retain the name of the Bill Gladstone Group.

Jim: Since we're talking about mailing, one of the problems that I see happen with brokers once they decide they want to start doing mailing, especially the brokers at the larger companies, is that all of a sudden management starts to get involved. Then management says things like, "Well, we don't want you to send out a mailer that looks like that. We don't want you to brand yourself; we want you to brand the name of the company, and not you."

Then I'm laughing at this going, "The broker is going to be paying for this out of their own pocket, and management is basically saying, 'We want control over how your mailers look. We want the company branded big, but you branded small, because remembering our company is more important than these people remembering you.'"

I'm just curious in your office if you have complete flexibility to mail whatever you want to mail to everyone.

Bill: It depends on how busy the people who watch this are in that particular week. We're supposed to follow the guidelines, and we do. We follow the font size and the color scheme for our company. That's not a problem for us because the colors aren't that bad, and you do have flexibility.

We used to have to use black and red. In the presentation I did this morning, we used orange and green. Some of the stuff is probably a little bit over the edge, but as long as we comply with the majority of it, the big stuff that is easily noticeable, nobody bothers us, and we're OK with that.

It works well because we like to have creative design. We like to be in charge of our own destiny and not be told, like you say, if I'm going to spend my money on this, "Here is what I want you to have it look like." That's hard to take. I agree with that.

We find a compromise and then we do what we want, and nobody seems to bother us.

Jim: There is a guy who I'm coaching who works for one of the major firms right now. He's been trying to get approval for months from upper management on the kinds of things that he wants to send out, and they're just stalling and taking their time. He finally said, "You know something? I'm just going to start mailing. So if they've got a problem with it, they can bring it to me." Not to mention the fact that there's a good chance they're not going to see the mailers anyway, because they're not going to be on the recipient list.

People in upper management are not marketing people. Generally speaking, they're admin people who have maybe never even done a mailing campaign themselves. They don't understand advertising and marketing like this, but they do understand covering their rear end with their own upper management.

Ideally you want to have management on board with what you're doing here. Ideally you want someone who says, "Hey, as long as it looks good and it's professional, and it's sending out a good message, and it's making both you and the company money, thank you for spending your own money and doing something like this."

Ideally, that's the type of support that you want to have from whatever firm you're working for.

Bill: You know something? For everybody listening tonight, if you can't get that, then do what Jim has suggested, because you can beg for forgiveness. Sometimes it's better to get it done that way than to ask for permission, because that's how you get the stalling going on, and everything else, so just do it.

Jim: Yes, you might get a good year or two years of mailing under your belt before someone then asks you about it.

Bill: That's the way to get it done.

Jim: The odds of one of your building owners knowing the management person in your company, and then forwarding your mailer onto that person are slim. In addition, as long as they like your mailers, why would they even do this? My point is that you've got to get your marketing and your mailing out, because this is about you making money, and the company making money, so as long as your mailers look good and professional, I think it's great. But obviously there can be politics involved.

With this in mind, obviously mailing is a big part of your business, Bill, and it has been for years. What do you think would happen to the volume of your commercial real estate transactions if you suddenly stopped mailing everything out to your clients and prospects?

Bill: I think the first thing that I would have to do, probably, is to let my entire staff go. I couldn't afford to be in business, as I know what marketing has done for me.

Unfortunately, what I'm about to mention did not go anywhere, but we teamed-up with one of the guys from the local township. He likes our marketing. We send him everything, and he's a township manager. He calls me up one day and says, "Hey, you've got to talk to this guy. I'm sending him over right now. He's in my office."

The guy was with the post office. The U.S. Post Office was concerned that they're losing so much business to digital that they're trying to figure out ways to blend the two, so people don't leave the USPS system.

They were using what they called the Layar application, where if you look through it, it gives you the opportunity to look through something which is augmented reality. It triggers within your magazine or your newsletter, or whatever you're sending out, and you look at it through your smart phone. So when you do this, you can actually see motion and movement. All of a sudden on the cover of that magazine there is a sound byte embedded in that picture of me, and there's a video byte embedded in that picture, too, and Bill Gladstone then comes to life, and he starts talking and moving.

Then he actually gets into a car and drives off the cover of the magazine as you're looking at it through your smart phone!

That's the kind of thing that we were working on, but it just didn't seem to have the draw that we thought it would have, so we've stopped using it, and we've saved the money for something else. But there is a lot of that out there that you can go to and try to use for your own benefit, and it can work.

Jim: You talked about seeing yourself on the cover of the magazine driving the car off the edge of the magazine cover, and I thought that was something that people might have seen in the 1960s, with all of the hallucinogens that were going on at the time!

Bill: You know, we've gone beyond that now, Jim.

Jim: But now, those people can get it on their smart phone with certain apps and certain programming now instead.

Bill: You know, I remembered something else as we were talking about these creative marketing ideas.

There is a mall here in town, and I was working with a guy to do some medical deals. He didn't know brokers, and he came in and they bought the mall out of bankruptcy.

One day we were standing out front, and there's a Bass Pro Shop there. There's a big sign there, and he's got another big sign right in front of the mall. So he says, "Can I take you out for lunch?"

I said, "No, I don't usually eat lunch. Today's not a good day."

He said, "Then some other time."

I said, "No, I don't really eat lunch that much. I grab something on the run and try to keep moving, because that's my active time of the day."

He said, "Well, can I put your name up on the sign?"

I said, "That one?"

He said, "Yeah."

I said, "Yes, but let me call you back on that."

The sign is right on the side of Interstate 83. I said to one of my assistants who lives on that side of town over there, "When you come back tomorrow, take a look at that sign and tell me if it would look good if we had our own picture up there, because this guy is offering it for free."

That sign is a jumbotronic TV. It's a $450,000.00 TV set. When traffic on I-83 comes to a halt or moves slowly, what does everybody do? My assistant said, "They watch TV."

I called the guy up and I said, "I'll take you up on your offer." I may even still be up there now. He let me stay up there a lot longer than I thought, and I got phone calls.

There is a picture of me up there in kind of a caricature-type style. What we did was I was doing Gangnam dancing, four seconds to the left, and four seconds to the right, so it attracted everybody's attention. They knew what Gangnam dancing was. All of a sudden, my company name and the Bill Gladstone Group came up right after that. We were only on the screen for like ten seconds, but I've got to tell you, I've never had that many phone calls, and people talk to me about it when they see me.

They would call me up and say, "I saw you on the sign." I'm thinking, "What sign?" Then I realized what they were talking about.

It gets back to how creative you can be. I mean, you wake up in the morning and you say, "Wow! What kind of trouble can I get into today? What can I do that sets me apart?"

You come up with ideas, you brainstorm, maybe you talk to some people, whatever it is. All of a sudden, you get this idea. When he said, "Can I put you up on the sign?" I thought, "Oh my God! Sure, and I like signs with motion, and I knew that the sign had motion up there."

Just push yourself to think because anything you look at, anything you stumble across, any mailer you do can give you a great idea to take it to the next step. I can't encourage people more, because I think people have the ability to think these things through.

You're just so rushed. You're running. You're trying to keep your face, your name, and anything about you in front of other people. I just think that's so important.

Jim: You talked about more people being able to see you on the sign in slow traffic. That may be the only time in your life when bad traffic has been a great thing for you, right?

Bill: Yes. How can I create more congestion?

Jim: There you go!

We talked earlier about how it's easy for brokers to just kind of look around and see what's going on in the office, and kind of do what everybody else is doing. When is it OK for brokers to follow what they see other brokers doing, and when does it become costly for them to do this?

Bill: I think the answer I would give you there is that it's OK to follow other brokers when you are following the brokers who are making the money. You know, yes, I make money here, but there are other brokers who make good money here, too. We all have different styles.

You take a look at Broker A. You take a look at Broker B and then Broker C. Then you say, "OK, who seems to have the style that I'm the most comfortable with?"

I've got a guy who I love to do deals with. He loves to work on deals with me right here in-house, and he makes a lot of money, too. His style is to get in and get out really quick. We hang around, we help the people with the little problems, because we think that is a value-add that no other broker is going to provide. But his style is to get in.

He knows I'll do the clean-up, so he moves on. He probably does three or four deals to my three deals or something like that averaged out over time. That may be your style. You can make money doing it if that's the way you are. It's not a right or wrong thing.

Just choose the broker you are the most comfortable being like, see what he does, and as long as he is making money, and good money, that could be somebody that you would want to follow.

We have one guy here. I've asked him, "Why do you always type your own letters?"

He said, "Because I can do it better than the admin people can."

I said, "I understand. So when you need it on Thursday, you pass it in on Monday. You do it over the weekend or you do it the Friday before and have it turned in on Monday. They give it back to you Monday afternoon and you work on it Tuesday. You give it back by Thursday, and it's perfect and it goes out because you've given it enough corrections, but you haven't spent the time to be your own typist." He's the highest paid typist in the house. He's not making great money, but as far as typing goes, he's making more than they are.

That's the kind of broker I would not follow.

Jim: I've got to mention something here. When you just told that story, I was thinking about this a couple of minutes ago when you were talking. For anybody who has been in this business for a while, whether it's been in one office, or in multiple offices throughout your career, there is often-times at least one person who you want to avoid when you go into the copy room, into the mail room, or into the lunch room. There's one person in the office who will love taking your time and telling you about all that's been going on with them, and telling you about all of the deals that have recently just blown up on them, or about what's wrong with this business, or about what's wrong with the world.

I remember there was a guy who worked for a company that I had worked for years ago, and he always had these strong opinions on things. I remember one time a bunch of guys went out together for lunch, and one of them came back and said, "You're not going to believe what he said this time!"

I said, "What?"

Then the guy said, "We were all getting into the elevator to go down for lunch, and he was late getting to the elevator, and then he got in. So one of the other guys near the elevator doors then pressed the button to make the doors close, and the other guy said, 'No, no. Don't ever do that! That actually slows down the elevator doors from closing instead of speeding them up.'"

As if anyone would ever do the research to determine that this was true!

He's one of these guys who thinks he knows everything, including the way that the engineers put the elevator together.

In addition, I think that brokers need to be careful on things like social media nowadays, because there are so many brokers out there who normally would never have an audience, but now they can get on social media, and get into the groups they want to, and start posting stuff that can just suck more time out of you...like arguing whether some app or software program deserves a three-and-a-half-star rating, or a four-star rating.

In the old days, they would have to put together their own email list and build a list to send to. But now, anybody can just get in and join a social media group, and begin pontificating about their own opinions to thousands of people.

You've just got to be careful. If you're doing social media, make sure it's something that is going to be making you more money, as opposed to just chit-chatting about everyone's opinions among brokers.

Alright, Bill. So you have bobblehead dolls that look like you that you have manufactured, and you give them out to people as promotional items. This is probably the greatest example of stepping outside the box that I've ever seen in commercial real estate brokerage.

So what was it that had you begin doing this?

Bill: My team and I try to brainstorm and come up with new ideas.

I had an assistant, who was not a great assistant, believe me, and she's no longer here, but she was sitting with us and she said, "Why don't we have a bobblehead?"

I looked at her and I said, "You're out of your mind! Why would we do a bobblehead doll of me? It's just so egotistical. Why would you do that?" Then we got away from talking about the subject.

Then I was at home that night having dinner with my wife and my youngest daughter and I said, "You've got to hear this one. Someone on my team said that we should do a bobblehead doll of me for marketing."

My wife and my daughter almost fell out of their chairs. They thought it was hilarious! They couldn't believe that we had come up with that idea. They thought it was the greatest idea they had heard in a very long time.

I said, "Really? I just don't see it." I thought about it, and I think Ronald Reagan was a good modern example of this in the sense that he got people to like him and understand him, because he could make fun of himself. People like people who can roll with the punches and make fun of themselves when it's appropriate to do so. You're then getting down in the trenches and you're getting closer to your people. It goes back to what you said about building the bond.

I thought about that again, and it took me some time, but we finally ordered 1,000 bobbleheads from China. They came in and we passed them out at closings. We sent them to people through the mail when they did leases with us. Once they did a transaction with us, we sent the bobblehead to them. At closing, we would take pictures of them with the bobblehead, and then we blew the pictures up. We photoshopped the pictures and we framed them, and then we sent the pictures to the people.

In fact, today I was talking to an attorney and he said, "Bill, thanks for the picture of me and my clients along with the bobblehead." It's just a picture, but I've seen those pictures with the bobbleheads in it because it's a memory of that closing. It's a memory of the lease in the lawyers' offices and in the engineers' offices, and in businesspeople's offices for years to come. Five years later I still see the pictures and I still see the bobbleheads, because on each bobblehead, when we pass them out at a settlement, or we send them through the mail when a lease is transacted, we put a personal message on each one for them. "You did a really nice job. Thanks for all the help and guidance you supplied." We make them feel good, and they put that bobblehead right in their office on their shelf, or on the edge of the desk, and it just sits there. But other people come in and they see it.

I know this because I was in a friend's office today and I saw that he had a bobblehead in there. I said, "That's really cool. I've got one, too."

I was going out the door one day and the UPS guy was coming into my office and he said, "I know you."

I said, "How could you know me? We've never met."

Then he said, "You're that little doll on all of those desks downtown."

"Alright," I said, "I like you!"

I understand. That's how it grew.

We kept putting out more of the bobbleheads, but only for closings and leases. We just ran out of them. We knew it was coming, so we ordered another 500. I don't think we ordered 1,000, because by the time we got rid of the first 1,000 bobbleheads, I had aged a few years. My hair was no longer jet black. It had gotten some grey in it.

Jim: And you're not using a Blackberry anymore, which was in the original bobblehead's hand.

Bill: That's right.

Jim: You needed to update your phone.

Bill: That's right. As you look at it, other than the fact that he's now showing my hair as being almost all white, which I object to, as you don't need to rush that process, he's got everything else right. He's got a little real estate sign out in front, with a place for people to put their own business card in, or to put my business card in.

It really is different.

The original bobblehead was $5.00 per unit and now it's $10.00 per unit. It now weighs more because it's a heavier product. It's a taller product, but it's a true bobblehead, and it's good. So we just started using that one.

I think in the next magazine you'll get, the cover will have "The Bobbleheads Are in Town" written on it, and you'll see what the new bobbleheads look like.

It's been very good as a marketing and promotion item. We get to closings and people just want to have their picture taken with the bobblehead, and so we do it. We love to do it, and we accommodate them. We bring a camera, and we also bring a cake and milk. We make a party out of it, because by then the work is all done, and this has worked very good for us.

Even the other brokers say, "Hey, I'd like to have a bobblehead!"

I say, "OK," and I know these brokers. So I say, "As long as I don't see that it's been run over in your parking lot, I'll send you one."

The ones who ask for it know they're never going to create one themselves. I have no problem giving it to them, because for them it's a keepsake and a memory of a deal, and that's as far as it's ever going to get, because they won't do it.

The ones who don't ask me for it, those are the ones who may end up doing it.

Jim: You mentioned Ronald Reagan earlier, and I remembered an interview that I heard with him, and he was saying that somebody once said to him, "How could you ever become President, having been an actor?"

Then Reagan replied with something similar to, "I don't understand how anyone could be President *without* having been an actor."

Bill: So true.

Jim: I want to mention to everybody, too, that you can see Bill's publications and his bobblehead doll on his website at www.BillGladstone.com, as well as see other resources that he has available there, too. You can see the magazine that he's been talking about, and the newsletters that he sends out, and that magazine is really something else! It's amazing when you get it in your hands in high-gloss print, but just take a look at it there and browse through all of the pages, and see the kind of detail that he's put together along with his team, and how impressive it really is.

I don't know any other type of marketing piece in our industry that's done by a broker or a brokerage team that can match that magazine, either in quality, or in cost! Your marketing budget is still in the neighborhood of $100,000.00 every year, correct?

Bill: Yes. But think about it. We spend about $60,000.00 on the magazine and we get paid back some of that with advertising. Then we have the newsletter, which costs about $2,000.00 a month, so that's another $25,000.00 a year there. But on that one, we don't get reimbursed at all through advertising. Then between the postcards and the flyers, we could easily get over the $100,000.00 mark, which would take into account some of the reimbursement that we get for the magazine ads.

Jim: We talked briefly a little bit earlier about video. Why don't you mention the kinds of videos that you've been doing for both marketing purposes, and for exposure on the internet?

Bill: I'd be glad to, Jim. The videos for us have been very challenging, even though we have our own equipment, and we have a guy here on our team who does the filming and brings one of his assistants who helps us with the lighting. The quality is pretty good, and I'm not worried about that, and I'm not worried about the sound. What we have trouble with is the fact that we're making educational videos.

For example, we'll bring in this CEO or a COO of a hospital. We'll bring in a developer who will sit there and they'll talk about medical build-to-suits. Now keep in mind I'm now in the presence of a hospital COO, and I'm also with one of the premier build-to-suit developers in the area, and I'm filming these guys talking to each other. Not only is it good for the audience, I think, but there's a certain relationship that is now starting to occur that no other broker has created. No other broker has taken these guys and coordinated with them to be in a meeting together, where they're going to have a video of them put up on the internet.

What we learned after doing that when we only got 75 views of that one, is that there are three things that are very important when doing video: providing educational material, which is not difficult to do, usually. Then the video needs to be short, and the other thing that's important is it has to have some sort of an entertainment component. People get bored easily. You lose the attention span. If they're not being entertained, you lose them. I bet you on that one where we had only 75 views, it probably got a little dry and boring. To help counteract that then you say, "OK, let's keep it short."

I think the best ones that I've seen on the internet that have gone viral, which is what we're shooting for, are the ones that have been maybe two-to-three minutes max. But when you have two people sitting there and you give them each three questions, I can tell you that you are at ten minutes easy, and that's just too long.

We've tried hard at this and we're going to come back to it. We're going to keep working at it, but it has to be short, it has to be educational, and I'm convinced that it has to have that entertainment component.

Jim: You have a team of five people, and obviously you're involved in making listing presentations. I'm just curious, since you've got expertise within this arena along with your team, do you have any recommendations to people in terms of how to make more effective listing presentations?

Bill: Yes, I can offer a couple of them. For the listing presentations, we turned to video. I got tired of PowerPoint and I got tired of going to PowerPoint presentations where people read to me off of the screen. It just annoys me to no end to have someone read to me what I can already read for myself. I don't have a problem if they will enhance it or expound upon what is already written up there, so I can hear them and read at the same time, and that's what really turned me away from PowerPoint. It's too easy for people to take the easy way out. They will just put slides up there and then read them to you, and I think that's what really irritates me.

Why are you doing this to me? Why are you trying to irritate me by not teaching me anything other than what I can read for myself if I just sat here and thumbed through your presentation?

So we said, "Let's go to the next step. Let's go to video for our presentations." When we've done video presentations, they've been very well-received.

I was approached by the county commissioner in one of the two counties that I work in. He said, "Listen, we want a presentation. We're having a beauty contest here, and we want you to participate."

I said, "OK. How long do I have?"

He said, "Forty-five minutes." Well, three calls later I was down to ten minutes, with him asking me, "Can you do this in ten minutes?"

I said to him, "I can do it in two minutes. You tell me what you want and I'll deliver what you want."

He said, "Ten minutes would work." So I show up and I'm sitting outside waiting for the other brokerage teams. I think there were three or four of us. I knew that we were in good shape, because everybody was sitting there with their paper presentations. There were the commissioners and there were a couple of other people in there, too. There were six or seven booklets, or whatever it was. We showed up with a projector and they had a screen. That's what we did.

When we got in there, we put the presentation up on the screen, and instead of passing out booklets and going through that whole thing of trying to tell people where to look in the book, I was standing there and I said, "Hello. This is Bill Gladstone, and I'm with the Bill Gladstone Group of NAI CIR. I want to introduce you to my partner." I took my right hand and I pointed to the screen. The projector goes on, and there I am on the screen. So now you've got virtual me, and then you've got the real me.

So the virtual me and the real me then had a dialogue back and forth together. I would walk around the room and I'd look back and say, "Bill, what do you think?"

We timed it right. We had to practice, but we timed it right. We gave them the same information, but we made it entertaining. That ten minutes turned into them now giving us 45 minutes, and we got the listing.

Jim: That's great! You bring up a really important point, because I think that so many brokers make the mistake of thinking that they're only in the information delivery business. While that is very important, ideally you need to recognize that you need to be in the entertainment business also, because people oftentimes make very boring business presentations.

We talked earlier about the importance of differentiating yourself as a broker, or as a brokerage team. If you're just standing there delivering information similar to, "These are the number of buildings that have sold in the last six months, and this is the average price per square foot…" you're not differentiating yourself, and you may actually be putting people to sleep.

But what you just talked about doing is phenomenal. The creativity of doing something like that with a video presentation in the room along with you… that's just going to grab people's attention, break up the monotony of their day, get them to smile, and it will differentiate yourself from the competition, too. With this in mind, brokers need to recognize that you really want to keep people stimulated, and you ideally want to add some humor into the situation, too. You want to keep them awake, and you want to make them feel like you're somebody personable who is humorous and fun to be around.

Why do you think that people turn to entertainment so much? It's because they want to get away from the monotony and into something that will entertain them or make them laugh. You ideally want to find that bridge of blending both information and entertainment into your presentations, along with having great presentation skills, too.

I think that's phenomenal, Bill, and I tip my hat to you on that one. With that in mind, where do you see your own business transitioning to now, with technology and marketing in the future?

Bill: We're headed more in the direction of technology. I've tried to work to bring younger brokers on to work with me. The money is good, but when they see the kind of money that I make, again, a lot of them don't want to work on weekends. Some of them don't want to work past 6:00 p.m. When you first get started in the business, I don't think anything has changed. You do what it takes, and if you have to work all day and all night, you do it to establish yourself. If you don't, I think you're still going to struggle getting into this business and making the kind of money you could make by maximizing your potential.

We've turned more away from trying to bring in more people to help me, and have now turned more instead towards technology. So we're investing in technology. In fact, my marketing group is a group of three. One person is the lead, and he has two assistants to help him on things.

We're trying to make our packages different. We're trying to incorporate video. We're trying to use different applications that we can find to do it with, other than just doing it on paper.

Today when we did our presentation we had a backup package that we left behind. It was paper, and it was what they needed, because we were talking about a bunch of different things. We had them all in there and they had the booklets, but I said, "Let's just focus on the screen." Today we did it with just slides. It wasn't a PowerPoint; it was just regular slides that we had used. They were digital slides, but not through a PowerPoint display.

That's the direction I want to go in. We've done displays, and instead of hooking the laptop into the projector, we've hooked the iPad into the projector. We can get right online and we can go into the aerials. We can do the ground photography, and it's different, because the iPad moves much faster. You can just keep flipping through the pictures very quickly.

They see you doing this, and that means a lot to them because they like to be associated with cutting-edge people. It's not only the content, but it's the process, too.

We're still exploring other ways of how we can use technology to our advantage, but so far, it's really mostly the laptop and the iPad. But I'm sure that will even change as time goes on.

Jim: So you're someone who is a member of both SIOR and CCIM. With this in mind, what recommendations do you have for brokers around getting interested in or joining and getting involved in either of these two organizations?

Bill: When I joined them when I first got into the business, I went to get my CCIM, and I said, "I have to do this because I have to do two things. First of all, having the CCIM after my name, for some people, will establish credibility." We had no CCIMs in the market at that time, or maybe there were just one or two.

Then I said, "It will not only give me the credibility having the CCIM designation after my name, but we've got people in this office today who can't even use a financial calculator." When you sit down and you have a client and you say, "Look, let's do an IRR," or, "Let's do a present value calculation," and nobody else in the office can do it, or only one or two other people can do it, you've now established that you have information that you can use to your own advantage that other people can't even use.

The best that they can do when you're doing present value is they will do an average. But it doesn't take into account the time value of money. This is not done overnight. You don't become a CCIM on a Thursday, and all of a sudden the whole market explodes in front of you on Friday. It takes time, but once you've done that, and I was very fortunate because back at that time for SIOR, if you already had your CCIM, you could use that for your educational requirement, and then you were still required to have your production.

I got busy on my production to get the amount that I needed, and I got the SIOR, which again, I'm now one of the only brokers in the market who had it. It's a point of differentiation. There are a lot of SIORs, more so now than there used to be, but there are only a couple of CCIMs, because educationally that is a harder task to accomplish. From a point of differentiation, now I can tell people that I've got some good financial knowledge that I can help them with, and I've also got the production to back it up, because with SIOR, there is a big production requirement. Even in our market, which is a small market, it's still a sizable task to get some stuff done, but when you have that behind you, you are set apart.

And you learn. There can't be anything more pleasing than to learn new concepts that you can use to help people solve their real estate problems. I mean, you are a service provider. You are bringing a solution to a problem and you have no problem doing that, because you are now armed with some tools that a lot of other people in your market probably don't have.

Jim: So in summing up, can we say that if a commercial broker isn't doing a good job of marketing in their business, that they're probably costing themselves a lot of money?

Bill: Absolutely. I mean, just to give you an idea here, in my business here, and I've cut my staff, I used to have seven assistants and I could keep them all busy. But again, when you start out you'll get one assistant, or maybe two. My overhead was extremely high. My overhead now has dropped from half a million a year down to $300,000.00, and payroll and marketing were my biggest expense.

Right now I probably have about $200,000.00 in payroll and about $100,000.00 in marketing, so I'm at around $300,000.00 to $325,000.00 in total.

Think about it like this. I don't make any money until I make one dollar more than $300,000.00. I get the privilege to start paying taxes when I make that first extra dollar, and yet I can well exceed that.

You can say, "Well, OK, Bill. What about if you didn't have the overhead and you scaled your marketing down?"

I was already at that point before I ever hired people to do these things for me and develop a marketing program. So when you don't have a team of people, you will not have the expenses, but you will not have the income either. If you develop a strong marketing program and you get your name out there, you'll get more people to choose from, and you'll have x amount of expense. Your own income dollars will be far greater than they would be if you didn't have the marketing, and I can't stress that enough, Jim. I know that from experience, because I started out one way and I ended up another way. I choose to stay the way I ended up, because my income is now much greater.

Jim: That's why the biggest companies in the world do a huge amount of marketing. I mean, can you imagine car companies if they didn't do any advertising on TV, or in magazines? How would you know what cars you should be looking at when it's time to buy or lease? They create this image of themselves in your mind such that you already know which cars you want to test drive when you're out there looking for a car.

You want to create that image in people's minds so that they're already impressed with who you are as a professional, they feel that you have the knowledge to guide them as their ideal consultant or advisor, and they are already interested in working with you before they ever have their next commercial real estate requirement. That's what powerful marketing can do for you through doing things like mailing and publishing videos, and you want to embrace this, because it will make you a lot more money.

We now have a question from Jason. Jason, please state your question.

Jason: First of all, thank you Bill for being on the teleconference tonight. I really enjoyed it and I learned a lot from it. My question for you is that you mentioned that you have five team members. Could you define the roles of each of those five team members?

Bill: Absolutely. Keep in mind that I am one of the members. I am the sales guy, and I'm the only sales guy. I have an administrative assistant who takes care of all of my paperwork. She writes all of my contracts and does everything. We've taught her how to do that. She does the addendums and everything, Jason, because that is minutiae to me that I should not be involved in, so I can focus more on being with my clients.

With the other three people, Chuck heads up the marketing. He handles the digital marketing, the traditional marketing, and the object marketing, and he assigns it to the two ladies who work for him. They divide up the work according to who is going to do the graphics, and who is going to do the things in marketing that are not associated with the graphics.

When I tell Chuck what to do, I give him a deadline, and the packages, the CDs, and whatever I need done are on my desk the night before or the day before. That's how we do that.

We have employee handbooks here, too. They need to be updated now, but everybody knows what their job description is.

Jason: One last question. The content, for instance, in your newsletter... is that all exclusively from you? Do any of your team members write anything, or is that all written by you?

Bill: For the newsletter, no. It used to be all me, but it's not anymore. I don't have time to write. We want 1,200 words. We want it to be quantified, not just qualified. It can't be blue sky. It can't be something I write. I read it and sometimes I'll send it back to the people and say, "Could you add another example?" Or, "Could you do this or that?", and they will give us some pictures sometimes, or some charts. We'll do that. The rest of it is all our listings, and marketing puts all of that in. I don't get involved with that because I just don't want to.

Jason: So the 4,000 people who get the newsletter and the 4,000 people who get the magazine, are those all the same 4,000 people?

Bill: A lot of them are, yes.

Jason: OK. All right. Thank you very much.

Bill: You're welcome, Jason, anytime.

Jim: Thanks for the question, Jason. We have another question from Louis. Louis, please go ahead.

Louis: Good evening, gentlemen. Thank you both for your time and Bill for your very informative presentation.

Bill: Thank you.

Louis: I wanted to go ahead and ask you, if you had to advise a beginning agent with a limited budget, how much to set aside so that they can move forward with some type of marketing plan, and what to maybe concentrate or focus on specifically to maximize the return on those dollars, how would you advise them?

Bill: Good question, Louis. My comment to that would be to start with a one-page newsletter. Make it simple. You could write it yourself if you have time, or maybe you could find somebody who is an accountant to write an article on taxes, or tax obligations, or tax deductions at the right time of the year. That's what I do, because I don't have time to write it anymore.

Make it really simple, and try to keep yourself uninvolved, because if you are a beginning agent and you need to start, you need to focus on your sales. One of the things, for example, when we were talking about the magazine, is we outsource that entire thing. The articles I read for content, and the marketing team then proofreads it. Then we send it off to a professional proofreader.

The photo on the cover is done by somebody outside. I'm told when to show up and where to be, and that's it. Then I just leave, and then Chuck and the photographer figure it out. Sometimes we have sidebars put in. If we need a sidebar we call up the person who does sidebars for us, then we send the files down to the publisher.

I try to stay uninvolved, and that keeps me focused on what I'm supposed to be doing: selling. It's the same thing with a single-page newsletter. I would say that traditional marketing is a single-page newsletter, because not everybody right now is into the digital. A lot of people in their 50's and 60's who are decision makers may be more in tune to seeing something done professionally in print, than they would be to seeing it done digitally.

With the magazine, Jim is absolutely right. I could send that out and save a lot of money if I sent it out online, but when you put that in your hands and you feel it, and you touch it and you look at it, and it's glossy and it's done professionally, the crease is right, the staple is right, and everything is done well, and we pay for that, it's much more meaningful. I would suggest that you try that one-page newsletter. Make it simple, but get your picture on there and make sure that it goes across their desks.

Jim: That was a good question, Louis. Thank you very much.

Louis: Thank you. Just one more thing. Is there anything else you would allocate to marketing if you had a few extra dollars besides the newsletter... for a new agent?

Jim: What about postcards, Bill?

Bill: I was thinking about that. You know, I love personal marketing. Louis, what you could do is you could do a postcard of yourself. That just opens up all sorts of possibilities of what you could be doing on the front of that postcard. You could give somebody a good visual of who you are and how talented you are. Maybe it's a picture of you selling the Empire State Building. Again, that is more of a cliché, but just brainstorm on it. Put a picture of yourself right there as bold as life, and send it out for whatever it costs to a couple of hundred people. Make a statement and use the back of the postcard, too.

I'm not quite sure what you would put on there, because I haven't done that in a while. I know one time we did a postcard with me and two of my assistants. We dressed up as Moe, Larry, and Curly of The Three Stooges, and it was hilarious! You couldn't tell that it was me, and it really looked like them.

We put that on the front of a postcard and we had something catchy. We went over to a golf course and we had someone come over and take pictures of us while we were practicing. We put the tag line on the back. We got more calls out of that. People called and said, "Don't quit your day job," and people just connected with us. It was actually worthwhile doing, because those were people who we wouldn't have, in the normal course of business, really had the time to contact, but it was so important to do.

Louis: How about a "just sold" postcard with the listing, and then maybe on the back have personal information, or something to that effect. Do you think that would work?

Bill: I would take it a step further, Louis. I would put you on the postcard. Make that statement. Take that step. Don't use your listing, and don't talk about your listing. You are the real estate professional, and somehow you are going to have to get comfortable with it. Again, that is sometimes easier said than done.

Put yourself on there doing something real estate-connected. As I'm talking to you right now, I don't know what that is, but move away from the traditional. Become a little bit more of a contrarian and put something out there that the people aren't expecting.

Jim: Let me just mention something here, Bill.

Bill: Sure.

Jim: Something that I always teach people to do...because ideally you want to occupy that position in people's minds that you are the expert with the answers. You are the consultant/advisor who they can trust. Oftentimes I mention that on one side of the postcard you can ask a question of them to get them thinking. For example, "What's the difference between a net and a gross lease?" Or, "What could happen to you if your tenant isn't insured?"

Then you flip it over, and on the other side of the card you can provide the answer as the expert. You begin to frame this over time that Louis or whoever the person is, is the ideal person who is in their head answering important questions for them. This helps to then brand you as someone who understands what they're thinking about and provides them with the answers, which is a great place to be occupying within their minds.

So consider doing something like this also.

Louis: Great idea! Thank you so much.

Jim: Alright, man. Thank you for the question.

Bill, I just want to say thank you so much for being on the call tonight. You were wonderful. Do you have anything that you want to say as we move forward towards completion?

Bill: I think enough has been said. I think it's time to let the people go.

Jim: "Let my people go!"

Bill: I'm sitting here trying to think, "Could I sit here and listen to myself for an hour and a half?" Oh, boy! Maybe I've put these people through too much, but I've enjoyed it, Jim. I appreciate it. I always enjoy doing this with you, and I think the questions from Jason and Louis were excellent. I hope that people find success with it.

Jim: Yes, and again, thanks to both of them for their questions.

This concludes our presentation for this evening.

Epilogue

Well, there you have it. Five interviews with some of the greatest commercial real estate brokers in our industry. So the question for you then becomes, "What are you going to do right now to take your commercial real estate brokerage business to the next level?" With this in mind, if you're like most commercial brokers, you probably believe that you should be getting more prospecting done right now in your commercial brokerage business than you have been, and if this is the case for you, what are you going to do right now to make this happen?

Do you need to schedule the days and times for your prospecting within your contact management system well in advance, and then hold these times sacred? When you do this you'll definitely be getting more prospecting done, and you'll be constantly swimming in an abundance of great new leads.

Many brokers are getting their prospecting done only when they find that they have the time to do it, so when prospecting isn't your first priority, you'll never get a great amount of it done. You'll always feel that you should be getting more of it done, but you'll never seem to find the time to do it.

Do you need to build better relationships with your people so that you get constant, repeat business from them, and so that they always want to work with you exclusively? Building the kinds of relationships with your clients that will lead to constant, repeat business for you during your career is where you want to be playing the game, otherwise you'll be stuck with only closing new business from the new leads that you've been developing from your prospecting, while your past clients will be closing their next transactions with your competitors, instead of with you.

If you're great at developing new leads for listings from your prospecting, but you're not good at closing the owners on listing their properties with you once you've developed these new leads, then you need to work on your presentation skills. Something is happening from the moment that you first identify the owner as a lead, all the way up through you asking them for the listing, that's causing them to list with your competitors instead of you. So you'll need to identify what this is and then correct it, so that you'll successfully begin landing more listings.

If you want to stand out in the minds of your clients and prospects as the best broker they could ever work with before they ever have their next commercial real estate need, then you'll want to be marketing to them and sending them mail at the minimum of one to two times every month. It's very difficult to stand out in your people's minds through prospecting alone, as all of your competitors will be doing the exact same thing, and when your clients and prospects are hearing from 10-20 other brokers via telephone calls before they'll ever hear from you again, this makes it very difficult for them to remember you.

With this in mind, if you want a great, simple formula for developing a constant, solid stream of great new leads within your brokerage business, be prospecting 10-12 hours every week, and be mailing to your clients and prospects twice a month, sending them solid, helpful information, and always be including a photo of yourself within your mailers.

In addition, if you find that you're getting bogged down in doing administrative and follow-up activities, and you find that this is keeping you from doing your prospecting and developing even more new brokerage business, you need to learn how to delegate better. So many brokers believe that they need to be doing everything all by themselves in our industry, and this is costing them a ton of money. So hire someone to work for you, even if it's just a virtual assistant who can work for you on an hourly basis in the beginning, then you can gradually give them more work when you have more activities to delegate to them.

Ideally, in putting all of this together, you want to focus on working within the arena of commercial real estate brokerage that you love doing. If you're the rainmaker, the one bringing in all of the business, you'll want to be focused on being in direct contact with the people that you want to be doing business with, and delegating all of the administrative and follow-up activities to other people. If your time when working on productive activities is worth hundreds of dollars an hour or more, and you can pay someone tens of dollars an hour to delegate activities to them and free up even more productive time for you, this is a great tradeoff of dollars for reclaiming back more of your productive time.

In moving forward, now that you've read this book, probably the best recommendation I can give you is to take the top 3-5 ideas that you've learned from this book, and begin implementing them into your brokerage business. These will be the top 3-5 ideas that you believe will have the greatest positive impact on your brokerage business if you just implement them. As long as we're going to be making changes in your business, we might as well begin by making the changes that you believe will have the greatest impact, and the ones that will begin making you the greatest amount of money. Then, once you've implemented these 3-5 changes into your business, you can then continue on in implementing even more of them.

In closing, I thank you for reading this book. I hope that it has given you both ideas and new insights on how you can improve your brokerage business, and I hope that it has created a burning desire within you to make this happen.

If you'd like additional information, please visit my website at www.CommercialRealEstateCoach.com. There you'll find articles and free training videos on subjects like prospecting, scripting for prospecting, what you should say to the receptionist, what you should say to the decision maker, and how to leave powerful voicemail messages that will compel more decision makers to call you back. In addition, you'll see videos on how to get more listings, and you'll see videos on subjects like power marketing, closing, persuasion, and on how to become even more powerful with your presentation skills.

If you're ever interested in one-on-one coaching to help you to take your commercial brokerage business to the next level, you can let me know through my website, and with that being said I wish you all the best of success as you move forward within your commercial real estate brokerage business!

About the Author

Jim Gillespie is America's Premier Commercial Real Estate Coach^{sm}. After having spent 20 years as a commercial real estate agent himself, Jim recognized the need to bring outstanding coaching to commercial real estate brokers, so he then created the commercial real estate coaching industry.

Jim also recognized that there's oftentimes very little sharing of success strategies within commercial real estate offices, as top agents often don't want to reveal their strategies for fear of creating even greater competition for themselves. In addition, many agents find that there is very little training being made available for them within their own companies, and they're oftentimes told just to pick up the phone and begin calling people.

Recognizing this, Jim began making one-on-one coaching available to commercial agents, and during his calls he instills within the agents the techniques, approaches, and success strategies of the best commercial real estate agents in the business, and he holds his coaching clients accountable to make sure that they implement these strategies.

In addition, Jim recognized the need to conduct interviews with top commercial real estate brokers, so that commercial brokers everywhere could learn from these top agents, and to date Jim has now done more than 140 interviews with these truly outstanding brokers.

Jim's attitude has always been that if you're determined to take your commercial real estate brokerage business to the next level, and you're coachable, willing to take direction, and willing to do whatever is necessary to get there...you can achieve everything that you want to in this business directly through one-on-one coaching.

For more information, including gaining access to Jim's more than 70 free commercial agent training videos, you can visit Jim's website at www.CommercialRealEstateCoach.com.

Made in the USA
San Bernardino, CA
14 May 2018